Quotable Scots

Quotable SCOTS

by
Carole MacKenzie

MAINSTREAM
PUBLISHING
EDINBURGH AND LONDON

First published in Great Britain in 1995 by
MAINSTREAM PUBLISHING COMPANY
(EDINBURGH) LTD
7 Albany Street
Edinburgh EH1 3UG

ISBN 1 85158 576 1

A catalogue record for this book is available from the
British Library

Typeset in Sabon by Litho Link Ltd, Welshpool, Powys, Wales
Printed and bound by WSOY, Finland

To Scot, so that he will never forget the land
of his birth

INTRODUCTION

Ostensibly a small nation, Scotland has produced a
high proportion of men and women who have
made their mark on world history. This book
gathers together some of the most memorable
things said by and about Scots and their native
country.

The native Scots talent for self-expression has
produced an array of internationally acclaimed
authors, such as Robert Burns, Sir Walter Scott
and J.M. Barrie. Other well-known Scots, such as
Alexander Graham Bell, found fame and fortune
only when they left their homeland. Yet, whatever
their final destination, Scots remain essentially
Scottish, and there has always been a strong
emotional undercurrent drawing the heart back
home.

Some of the observations you will find in this
collection were made by non-Scots – Dr Samuel
Johnson, for example, had plenty to say about
Scotland and its people. Lord Byron, however, is
included here as a Scot. Although he is often
referred to as an English Romantic poet, he was
the son of a Scottish heiress, and he spent most of
his formative years in the northern counties of
Scotland. Byron summed up the Scottish character
well when he wrote in Don Juan:

> But I am half a Scot by birth
> And bred a whole; and my heart
> flies to my head.

The occasion when contemporary Scots are at
perhaps their most passionate is a rugby
international against England at Murrayfield.
R.H. Bruce Lockhart, writing in 1937, notes:

> In this emotional tumult there is something of the spirit
> of Bannockburn.

Although it takes contests against the Auld
Enemy to evoke this type of Celtic enthusiasm,

Scots follow all their leisure pursuits with similar fervour, humour and with the endearing quality of being able to laugh at themselves. The Rangers footballer Ally McCoist enthuses that:

> The best thing in football is scoring goals – and I'm a top goalscorer.

Scots are also fiercely patriotic, and as we move towards the twenty-first century, politicians of all parties will lay the foundations for a new Scotland, perhaps devolved or independent. Even when on the campaign trail, our MPs keep their sense of humour. Winnie Ewing, Scottish Nationalist Member of the European Parliament, says thankfully:

> We've only had three rude signs so far this time.

Among contemporary Scots, personalities such as Robbie Coltrane, John Sessions, John Gordon-Sinclair, Emma Thompson, Marti Pellow, Jim Kerr, Annie Lennox and Billy Connolly, to name but a few, have all won international acclaim. But perhaps our most famous son is Edinburgh-born Sean Connery, alias James Bond, who was memorably described by an American magazine as:

> A great Scot who's banged more baddies and Betties than humanly possible.

Finally, the following quotation – James Watt's reaction on being offered a baronetcy – exemplifies one of the Scots' most distinctive traits, namely that they are slow to be impressed:

> Sir James Watt? Never.

ACTING

I just don't believe it.
Richard Wilson, *actor, receiving his Scottish BAFTA,*
1993

I just love my job.
Siobhan Redmond, *actress*

I enjoy the excitement of working on a well-
crewed and exciting picture. It's like a microcosm
of society that really works. Because nothing
works anywhere else.
Sean Connery, *actor,* International Herald Tribune, *1983*

It's going to be a happy ending – though he still
gets hung, drawn and quartered.
Mel Gibson, *actor, describing his acting role as Scottish*
hero William Wallace

I get enough gigs, along with corporate pre-match
entertaining at Easter Road, to pay up my NHS
prescriptions.
Gary Denis, *Edinburgh comedian,* Evening News, *1994*

A piece of camp old pish. It's a load of nonsense
really.
Forbes Masson, *actor, speaking of his latest comedy*
television series, 1994

I adore not being me. I'm not very good at being
me. That's why I adore acting so much.
Deborah Kerr, *actress,* Times, *1972*

Excuse me, ladies and gentlemen, I'm having a bit
of stage fright.
John Sessions, *actor, at a London theatre before fleeing*
into the wings, Sunday Express, *1995*

I used to lie about it, tell taxi drivers I was an
electrician. About two years ago I made up my
mind to stop denying it.
John Gordon-Sinclair, *admitting that he used to deny*
being an actor

The one thing you don't want to do is let them down. You're never late and you learn your lines till you're blue in the face, in case you drop them in it.
Phyllida Law, *actress, on the responsibilities of acting with family members, 1995*

I just had to sit down.
Dorothy Paul, *comedy actress, on hearing that she had won the Scottish BAFTA Light Entertainment Award, 1993*

I'm just the minder tonight. I shall watch her again on TV and get terribly drunk.
Kenneth Branagh, *actor, after his wife, Emma Thompson, had won the BAFTA Best Actress Award, 1993*

By the end I felt disgusting, but I think it was worth while to make my character authentic.
Clare Grogan, *actress, after portraying a homeless person on television, 1991*

The guy should be young – at least under 50.
Sean Connery, *actor, on being asked about the requirements of a new James Bond, 1992*

The essence of sitcom for us is the characters, not the situations. Eventually we said let us do it the way we want to or bugger off.
Forbes Masson, *describing his response to a script editor who tried to persuade him to write to formula*

ACTION

It is the mark of a good action that it appears inevitable in the retrospect.
Robert Louis Stevenson *(1850-94), writer*

I have spent a long life in improving the arts and manufactures of the nation. My inventions at present, or lately, give employment to the best part of a million people.
James Watt *(1736-1819), engineer, assessing his achievements*

The active car is much easier to drive, and when it hits a bump the car settles very quickly.
David Coulthard, *racing driver, explaining his preference for a car with active suspension*, Scotsman, *1994*

When we came to the end of the agenda and I handed them the letter saying I was going, there were tears in my eyes.
Wallace Mercer, *chairman of Hearts*, Scotsman, *June 1993*

Attitudes only change when we see the horrific consequences of our inactivity.
Kaye Adams, *writer, criticising the reluctance of governments to give cash to Third World countries, 1992*

The tension was released when one of the more intelligible Scottish officers spoke to them. So one friendly fire incident was averted.
Col. Robert Anderson, *Royal Army Medical College, describing a Gulf War incident in which a plane load of Scots reservists narrowly avoided being shot down by American fighters*, Scotsman, *1994*

ADDRESS

Edina! Scotia's darling seat!
Robert Burns *(1759-96), poet, 'Address to Edinburgh'*

Addresses are given to us to conceal our whereabouts.
Saki (H.H. Munro) *(1870-1916), writer, 'Reginald in Russia', 1910*

It was important for me to begin my address today in the Gaelic language.
Donnie Munro, *of Gaelic group Runrig, beginning his inaugural speech as 43rd Rector of the University of Edinburgh, 1991*

Work is the grand cure of all the maladies and miseries that ever beset mankind.
Thomas Carlyle, *(1795-1881), historian and essayist, rectorial address at Edinburgh, 1886*

You come of a race of men the very wind of whose name has swept to the ultimate seas.
J.M. Barrie *(1860-1937), novelist and dramatist, rectorial address at St Andrews, May 1922*

Scotland is renowned as the home of the most ambitious race in the world.
Frederick Edwin Smith, *Earl of Birkenhead (1872-1930), English lawyer and statesman, rectorial address at Aberdeen*

A D V I C E

If your morals make you dreary, depend upon it, they are wrong.
Robert Louis Stevenson

If you wish to preserve your secret, wrap it up in frankness.
Alexander Smith *(1830-67), poet*

Don't bless yourself on the park.
David Murray, *chairman of Rangers, to French footballer Basile Boli*, Daily Record, *December 1994*

One's prime is elusive. You little girls, when you grow up, must be on the alert to recognise your prime at whatever time of your life it may occur.
Muriel Spark, *novelist*, The Prime of Miss Jean Brodie

If he could learn to convey to the Scottish public desperate for a world-beating hero the natural warmth and wit of the city of his birth, he would be a winner all round.
David Feherty, *Irish golfer, advising fellow golfer Colin Montgomerie to relax*

If you can't fail, you can't do anything, and it was brilliant advice.
Emma Thompson, *recalling advice given to her by her father*

If the management are making merry, follow the golden rule of being slightly merrier. Then you'll survive.
Duncan McIntosh, *behaviour expert, giving advice for office parties*

No more last-gasp heartbreak.
John Colquhoun, *Hearts footballer, on the new attitude at Tynecastle*

Aberdeen [Football Club] needs guys who will hand out stick when needed. In fact, the Dons need a couple of bastards.
Stuart Kennedy, *Aberdeen and Scotland goalkeeper*

When you come back you would be well advised to bring your pyjamas and toothpaste.
Sheriff Ian Cameron, *warning an accused after her fourth drink-driving charge, 1990*

To find a friend one must close one eye. To keep him – two.
Norman Douglas (1868-1952), *novelist and essayist, 1941*

The best way to get the better of temptation is just to yield to it.
Clementine Stirling Graham (1782-1877), *writer*

. . . If you wish the pick of men and women take a good bachelor and a good wife.
Robert Louis Stevenson

In baiting a mouse-trap with cheese, always leave room for the mouse.
Saki (H.H. Munro), *'The Infernal Parliament'*

The ideal board of directors should be made up of three men – two dead and the other dying.
Tommy Docherty, *football manager, 1977*

No man practices so well as he writes. I have all my life long been lying till noon; yet I tell all young men, and tell them with great sincerity, that nobody who does not rise early will ever do any good.
James Boswell (1740-95), *writer*

Put all good eggs in one basket and then watch
that basket.
Andrew Carnegie (1835-1918), industrialist and
philanthropist

All I want to say, particularly to our partners . . .
is don't rush it, don't push it, because that isn't
going to help us get it through.
Norman Lamont, Chancellor of the Exchequer, referring
to the Maastricht Treaty

But if you happen to have any learning, keep it a
profound secret, especially from the men, who
generally look with a jealous and malignant eye on
a woman of great parts and cultivated
understanding. A man of real genius and candour
is far superior to this meanness. But such a one
will seldom fall your way.
John Gregory (1753-1821), doctor, giving advice to his
daughters, Scots Magazine, 1774

A G E

Being over 70 is like being engaged in a war. All
our friends are going or gone and we survive
among the dead and the dying as on a battlefield.
Muriel Spark, Memento Mori

Ladies, even of the most uneasy virtue, prefer a
spouse whose age is short of 30.
Lord Byron (1788-1824), poet

I've honestly not been too aware of my age until I
went to the doctor for a full check-up. He said I
had the heart of a young man – but you're not
young, you're forty.
Sean Connery, Evening Standard, 1971

Some reckon women by their suns or years.
I rather think the moon should dare the dears.
Lord Byron

I just pace myself these days. I'm 48 and I can't do it five nights a week any more or I will run into problems. My voice is the most important thing, obviously, and I treat it very carefully. You can't thrash your body as much as you could when you were younger.
Rod Stewart, *rock singer, explaining why a unique rock'n'roll voice is not wearing well, February 1993*

Age may have one side, but assuredly youth has the other. There is nothing more certain than that both are right except that both are wrong.
Robert Louis Stevenson

I'm sure that will be fun for people like you to write about.
Lulu, *singer, to reporter, who suggested she might still be strutting her stuff at 50, December 1993*

I don't see any great value in dwelling on it.
Sean Connery

The young have aspirations that never come to pass, the old have reminiscences of what never happened.
Saki (H.H. Munro)

This day I am 30 years old. Let me now bid a cheerful adieu to my youth. My young days are now surely over, and why should I regret them? Were I never to grow old I might be always here, and might never bid farewell to sin and sorrow.
Janet Colquhoun *(1781-1846), writer, diary, 1811*

I am just a few months older than *Coronation Street*, and a dedicated fan.
Lorraine Kelly, *TV presenter, 1993*

AMBITION

Playing for the Rangers is a fairy tale come true. My dad took me to my first Rangers game when I was nine and it's been my ambition to play for them ever since.
Ally McCoist, *Rangers footballer*

I want to be the Steve Davis of the 1990s.
Stephen Hendry, *snooker player, after winning the Embassy World Championship, 1990*

Fawlty Towers is the kind of thing I'd like to do.
Sean Connery, *admitting that he would like to do more comedy acting*, Woman's Realm, *1994*

It sounds like a fantastic opportunity to eat haggis, admire the scenery – and have lots of great sex!
Paula Yates, *TV presenter, admitting that she and her husband, Bob Geldof, would like to travel on the West Highland Railway, 1993*

AMERICA

There they are cutting each other's throats, because one half of them prefer hiring their servants for life, and the other by the hour.
Thomas Carlyle, *referring to the American Civil War (attrib.)*

It is a form of Arctic St Andrews.
Robert Louis Stevenson, *of Saranac Lake, New York, 1888*

America is the last abode of romance and other medieval phenomena.
Eric Linklater *(1899-1974), novelist,* Juan in America

Walking is an un-American activity.
Lord Kinross, The Innocents at Home, *1959*

Aye, they have a great population, viz., 21 millions of the greatest bores that the moon ever saw.
David Livingstone *(1813-73), explorer, letter, September 1852*

I love short trips to New York; to me it is the finest three-day town on earth.
James Cameron, *journalist and travel writer*, Witness, *1966*

A P P E A R A N C E

Too much lipstick. I really don't like women who
are over made-up.
*Tony Roper, playwright and comedy actor, on being
asked if there was anything he didn't like about women,
1991*

Call me an old square, but I like women to look
feminine. They tend to dress down, which I think
is unappealing.
Johnny Beatty, comedian

One of the most gratifying things about the
Duchess of Pork is that despite the diets, the
exercise and the personal trainer, the woman still
bulges in all the wrong places.
*Joan Burnie, of Sarah Ferguson, Duchess of York, Daily
Record, 1992*

A R C H I T E C T U R E

[T]here are many decorative features in Scottish
architecture, which might well be replaced by
others of antiquity yet just because we are Scotch
and not Greek or Roman we reject . . . In fact I
think we should be a little less cosmopolitan and
rather more national in our architecture.
Charles Rennie Mackintosh (1868-1928), architect

Adam, our most admired architect, is all
gingerbread, filigraine and fan-painting.
*Horace Walpole (1717-97), English man of letters, of
Scottish architect Robert Adam*

I endeavoured to render it a noble and elegant
habitation, not unworthy of a proprietor who
possessed not only wealth to execute a design but
skill to judge of its merit.
*Robert Adam (1728-92), architect, of his restoration of
Syon House, home of the Duke of Northumberland*

ART

For the really daring there's an exhibition of extremely tasteful pornography, which promises to examine 'the nature of commercial sexual representation'.
Peter Oldham, writer, reviewing an Edinburgh Festival art exhibition, 1992

Now it seems to be evident that there is a difference being an artist and having been an artist, and that the word artist strictly applies to the person who *persists in being* an artist.
J.D. Fergusson (1874-1961), modern Scottish painter

Art and religion first; then philosophy; lastly science. That is the order of the great subjects of life, that's their order of importance.
Muriel Spark

Those who plump their own over-upholstered bahookis on Scottish Opera's over-subsidised seats are more likely Tory voters than Wildcat customers.
Joan Burnie, columnist, arguing that the Wildcat Theatre Company deserves sponsorship

The most impressive work of art I have ever seen.
Sir Walter Scott (1771-1832), novelist and poet, praising Telford's Chirk Aqueduct on its completion, 1803

He is the man who has turned sloth into an art form, indolence into a political philosophy, inaction into a declaration of intent.
Sir Norman Fowler, Conservative politician, of John Smith, then Leader of the Labour Party

If the Tate can buy a load of old bricks then why not a beautiful natural peat stack?
Dr Finlay MacLeod, Gaelic historian and film producer, urging the Arts Council to make grants available to natural artists, Scotsman, 1994

AS OTHERS SEE US

O wad some Power the giftie gie us
To see oursels as ithers see us!
It wad frae monie a blunder free us,
An' foolish notion.
Robert Burns, 'To a Louse'

He has no vision in him. He will neither see nor
do any great thing.
Thomas Carlyle, of Thomas Babington Macaulay

No McTavish was ever lavish.
Ogden Nash (1902-71), American humorist, Hard Lines

Sour, stingy, depressing beggars who parade
around in schoolgirls' skirts with nothing on
underneath.
P.J. O'Rourke, American writer, of Scottish
characteristics, 'Foreigners Around the World', National
Lampoon, 1976

There was even a stall selling sex aids here one
week, until somebody noticed they weren't curling
tongs, like we'd thought.
Female shopper, Ingliston Market, Julia Clarke feature,
Daily Record

Macduff: O Scotland, Scotland . . .
O Nation miserable!
William Shakespeare (1564-1616), playwright,
Macbeth, c.1605-6

Cursed Jezebel of England!
John Knox (c.1513-72), Protestant reformer, of Queen
Mary I

John Byrne has taken great liberties with the story.
But it's a great story and I hope it'll make a great
film.
Robbie Coltrane, actor, speaking of his role in a
television dramatisation of Boswell and Johnson's journey
to the Western Isles

I listen to some actors being interviewed and I
think, what a bunch of absolute plonkers.
Phyllis Logan, actress, Mail on Sunday, 1993

Yes, I thought I wasn't mistaken. You've got a Glasgow walk.
A fellow Scot, walking in New York, recognising Jim Kerr, singer with Simple Minds

When he plays on snow, he doesn't leave any footprints.
Don Revie, *manager of Leeds United, of footballer Eddie Gray, 1970*

To some people I am rude and aggressive – they provoke about 50 per cent of it by their attitude to me. I can't go around with a welcome mat around my neck.
Sean Connery, Playboy, *1965*

You mentioned your name as if I should recognise it, but beyond the obvious facts that you are a bachelor, a solicitor, a freemason, and an asthmatic, I know nothing whatever about you.
Sherlock Holmes, in 'The Norwood Builder', by
Sir Arthur Conan Doyle (1859-1930)

The way he's losing his hair, he'll be the first bald guy ever to do impressions of Elvis Presley.
Graeme Souness, *footballer, of a teammate, 1984*

His mind was a kind of extinct sulphur pit.
Thomas Carlyle, *of Napoleon III*

You look hideously ugly with a cigarette, you smell revolting – and if I get my way you'll only be allowed to poison yourself and your family in the privacy of your own home.
Muriel Gray, *TV presenter and writer, on smokers*

His interests are limited to say the least. At home he never read anything in the newspapers but the sports pages.
Catherine Lockley, *daughter of Tommy Docherty, 1981*

In real life, I'm just a big plain Jane.
Andy Bell, *singer with Erasure*

A man with the vision of an eagle but with a blind spot in his eye.
Andrew Bonar Law (1858-1923), *Unionist politician, of Lord Birkenhead*

Take Boris Becker, which no self-respecting woman would. It isn't just his racquets which have a great deal of gut.
Joan Burnie

Wearing very tight, striped pants, he looked like a bifurcated marrow . . . like a pensionable cherub.
Clive James, of Rod Stewart in concert

I was annoyed by Rory Bremner doing an impression of me which makes me look like a complete moron. It's a terrible impression too.
Terry Christian, TV presenter, of Rory Bremner, Scottish impersonator

I got some stick for wearing it, so I decided to auction it to raise cash for a very worthy cause.
Marti Pellow, singer with Wet Wet Wet, auctioning his favourite suit for charity, 1993

The Villa chairman, Doug Ellis, said he was right behind me. I told him I'd sooner have him in front of me, where I could see him.
Tommy Docherty, 1970

A case of the doc calling the kettle black.
Jane Gordon, columnist, referring to Dr David Owen backing the Conservatives in the 1992 general election, Today, 1992

Pale and wearied, with a grey beard, wearing a bluish cap with a faded gold band round it, a red-sleeved waistcoat and a pair of grey tweed trousers.
Henry Stanley (1841-1904), *explorer, describing his first sighting of Livingstone when they met at Ujiji*

His bottom was that of any Scotch nobleman: proud, aristocratical, pompous, imposing.
Sir Lewis Namier (1888-1960), *historian, describing John Stuart, third Earl of Bute, First Lord of the Treasury*

A bigot and a sot, bloated with family pride, and eternally blustering about the dignity of a born gentleman.
Thomas Babington Macaulay *(1800-59), English writer, of James Boswell*

Maw, Paw and the weans looked like a family of hungry gypsies. Their clothes could have come from a jumble sale.
Sandra Ratcliffe, *describing singer Bob Geldof and family,* Daily Record, *1993*

He has a knee-jerk response to everything.
Alastair Campbell, *journalist, of Anthony Beaumont-Dark, Tory MP*

He was so mean, it hurt him to go to the bathroom.
Britt Ekland, *actress, on former partner Rod Stewart*

Anyone who puts themselves forward into public affairs cannot be too sensitive about the way they are described.
Ian Hamilton, *SNP candidate in European elections, who was labelled a thief when he stole (or, as he believed, reclaimed) the Stone of Destiny from Westminster Abbey*

No yawning, no sniggering, no mumbling of the hymns . . . could be the best thing that has ever happened to the Church of Scotland.
Kaye Adams, *welcoming the use of camcorders at weddings, 1993*

He has an attractive voice and a highly unattractive bottom. In his concert performances he now spends more time wagging the latter than exercising the former, thereby conforming to the established pattern by which popular entertainers fall prey to the delusion that the public loves them for themselves, and not for their work.
Clive James, *of Rod Stewart*

Dante without the poetry;
Irving without the mystery;
Mephistopheles without the fun.
Alan Dent, *of Sir John Reith, 1939*

What's that bald guy doing with three models?
*Tourist, to photographers in St James's Park, witnessing a
photo opportunity involving John Smith and his three
daughters just after his election as leader of the Labour
Party*

So this is your Scotland. It is rather nice, but
dampish and northern and one shrinks a trifle
inside one's skin. For these countries one should be
amphibian.
D.H. Lawrence *(1885-1930), English writer, letter, 1926*

A U L D   R E E K I E

The inhabitants of Edinburgh are forever calling
their beautiful city the modern Athens or the
Northern Oxford or the Scottish Wigan or
something that it isn't or, at least, has no business
to be.
James Bridie (O.H. Mavor) *(1888-1951), dramatist,*
One Way of Living, *1939*

You might smoke bacon by hanging it out of the
window.
Robert Southey *(1774-1843), English poet and writer,*
Journal of a Tour in Scotland in 1819

Football is too working class and fag-end for the
city, which is biased towards rugby.
Wallace Mercer, *on Lothian Region's plans for a green-
field site for Edinburgh's Premier League clubs*

A X I O M

After the game, bishops and pawns go back into
the same box.
Cardinal Winning of Glasgow, *after his elevation to
cardinal, joking that he hadn't forgotten he was a priest,*
Daily Record, *December 1994*

It has long been an axiom of mine that the little
things are infinitely the most important.
*Sherlock Holmes, in 'A Case of Identity', by **Sir Arthur
Conan Doyle***

A Scottish man is ay wise behind the hand.
***John Ray**, writer, 1670*

BANKING

It will lower staff morale, which is already at rock-
bottom. It is absolutely degrading.
*Spokesman for BIFU (the banking union), responding to
Royal Bank of Scotland staff complaints that they would
be given a toy monkey to put on their desk if they did not
rearch targets*

Local managers in some areas have gone mental.
Royal Bank of Scotland staff member

BARMAIDS

Barmaids are like priests, confession's part of the
daily round; surprise is beyond them, often even
interest.
***Allan Massie**, writer, One Night in Winter*

BEAUTY

Beauty in things exists in the mind which
contemplates them.
***David Hume** (1717-76), philosopher, Essays of Tragedy*

She walks in beauty, like the night.
Lord Byron

Perfect beauty is its own sole end.
***James Thomson** (1834-82), poet*

I always say beauty is only sin deep.
Saki (H.H. Munro)

Beauty and Truth, though never found, are worthy
to be sought.
Robert Williams Buchanan *(1841-1901), writer,*
To David in Heaven

B E D

In my experience, husbands who regularly buy
their ever-loving spouses lots of goodies are
extremely generous in bed . . . The trouble is that
the beds in which they are so munificent usually
belong to women other than their wives.
Joan Burnie, *responding to a survey which found that
husbands who rarely buy their wives presents are also
mean in bed*

Personally, I am a great believer in bed. In
constantly keeping horizontal, the heart and
everything else goes slower and the whole system
is refreshed.
Sir Henry Campbell Bannerman, *1900*

B E S T - L A I D   S C H E M E S

If the manager keeps saying, 'We'll win it, we'll
win it, we'll win it', eventually they [the players]
believe you.
Ally Macleod, *Scotland manager, before the World Cup,
1978*

History is too serious to be left to historians.
Iain Macleod *(1913-70), politician,* Way of Life

I just try to drink five or six glasses of wine a day,
which is twice the limit but, you know . . .
Rod Stewart, *singer,* Daily Mail, *1993*

BLANKETY BLANK

In our two previous games Rangers have stuffed us. That's the only way to describe it.
Joe Jordan, Hearts manager

You are a silly, rude bitch, and, since you are a potential breeder, God help the next generation.
Sir Nicholas Fairbairn (1933-95), Conservative politician, remark to young woman heckler, Daily Mail

To listen to some people in politics, you'd think 'nice' was a four-letter word.
Sir David Steel, Liberal politician, party political broadcast, 1987

There may be nicer ways to put this but I've found that when it comes to telling a few home truths plain speaking is always the best. Hibs are in the s***.
Andy Goram, former Hibernian and Scotland goalkeeper, 1991

Aye, I remember the Lam'nt lad. He's an arrogant little bugger, you know. I don't think he's fit for the job he's doing at all.
Harry Drever, former manager of the Bank of Scotland, Lerwick, of Norman Lamont, then Chancellor of the Exchequer, Mail on Sunday, 1993

I love to be treated like a woman. If some guy opens a door for me, I'll be the first to thank him – and if he doesn't I'll be the first to say, 'You ignorant git.'
Sharleen Spiteri, of rock band Texas, 1993

He should be put to death, why rise above it?
John Sessions, using a four-letter word while blasting a critic who had given him a bad press, Radio 4 interview, 1995

Whatever the state-of-art backing, you can't disguise the fact that it's Rod hollering away and talking through his cock.
Music critic, of Rod Stewart, Sounds

BONKERS

The reason they think I'm bonkers is because I
have original views and speak my mind.
Sir Nicholas Fairbairn

I told one of the couples they were a pair of
nutters for wanting to get married there. But they
said it was so romantic because *Hamlet* was filmed
there.
*Revd Sam Ballantyne, who was reported to Aberdeen
Presbytery for marrying a couple at Donnottar Castle,*
Scotsman, *1993*

Roses are red
Violets are blue,
I'm a schizophrenic
And so am I.
Billy Connolly, comedian

BORDER

This queer compromise between fairyland and
battleground which is the border.
H.V. Morton (1892-1979), English writer, In Search of
Scotland, *1929*

BORES

Let's face it, it's like watching a tea-towel dry on a
radiator.
John Sessions, describing a TV soap

An England win would mean having to listen to
Jimmy Hill and company for another 24 years –
the best way of guaranteeing Scotland gets
independence.
*Chris McLean, SNP spokesman, before England's
appearance in the 1990 World Cup*

If Everton were playing at the bottom of my
garden, I'd draw the curtains.
Bill Shankly (1913-81), manager of Liverpool

BOXING

I felt I was fighting for Scotland, and my true happiness lies in the fact that I did not let Scotland down.
Benny Lynch (1913-46), *boxer, after winning the world flyweight title, 1935*

If he beats me, I'll be the first one to congratulate him.
Ken Buchanan, *former world lightweight boxing champion, before his fight with Roberto Duran, 1972*

A black day in my life.
Ken Buchanan, *eating his words*

BRAG

York was, London is, but Edinburgh shall be
The greates o' the three.
Thomas the Rhymer, *thirteenth century*

Parole, parole, nothing but words. The Scots will boast but rarely perform their brags.
David Riccio (1533-66), *Italian courtier and musician*

This city needed something to believe in – so I gave it me.
Jock Wallace, *manager of Leicester City*

I think there is a blossom about me of something more distinguished than the generality of mankind.
James Boswell, London Journal, *1763*

The city has two great teams – Liverpool and Liverpool Reserves.
Bill Shankly

I've had some good shouting contests with several refs because they give as good as they get, and we finish the best of friends afterwards.
Lou Macari, *footballer, 1977*

According to this most useless survey, men think about sex every six minutes, dirty pigs! But they actually manage to do something about it twice a week.
Joan Burnie, on a sex survey, 1992

I've been in more courts than Bjorn Borg.
Tommy Docherty, 1981

To do things is not half the battle. Carlyle is wrong about this. To be able to tell the world what you have done, that is the greater accomplishment.
Andrew Carnegie

You don't get any bigger than the quarter-finals of the FA cup.
Alex Ferguson, manager of Manchester United

Pompous the boast, and yet a truth it speaks.
A 'modern Athens' – fit for modern Greeks.
James Hannay, of Edinburgh, Edinburgh Courant, 1860

I'm no angel, but I've never kicked anyone deliberately.
Billy Bremner, footballer, 1967

The crowd think he is posturing, call him 'big head'.
Arthur Rowe, author, of Billy Bremner, Encyclopedia of Association Football, 1960

In Ireland and in the mountains of Scotland the moonlight has a sharper edge to it.
H.V. Morton, In Search of Scotland

Scotchmen seem to think it is a credit to them to be Scotch.
W. Somerset Maugham (1874-1965), A Writer's Notebook, 1949

When Billy [Connolly] meets people they want to upstage him, and there is no way anyone will manage that.
Malky McCormack, cartoonist and musician

There's nothing I can't win now. Bring on the
world . . . I can rule it.
Stephen Hendry, *after winning the UK snooker title,*
1989

BRITISH

The British have always been so anti-analysis – in
every sense of the word.
Sean Connery, Evening Standard, 1972

BUSINESS

Everyone lives by selling something.
Robert Louis Stevenson

Avarice, the spur of industry.
Adam Smith (1723-90), *economist and philosopher*

If the Tory party were a commercial company, the
Royal Bank would shut it down as insolvent.
Robin Cook, *shadow Trade and Industry Secretary, 1993*

Perpetual devotion to what a man calls his
business is only to be sustained by perpetual
neglect of many other things.
Robert Louis Stevenson

We want to help not hinder business.
George Robertson, *Labour politician, calling for a*
Scottish Assembly

Football is similar to industry. All we're doing now
is reaping the rewards for the lack of investment.
David Murray

Mr Morgan buys his partners: I grow my own.
Andrew Carnegie, 'Hendryck, Life'

There is no doubt the biggest challenge, the most
demanding design work had to be making dresses
for Jimmy in drag.
Gina Fratini, *dress designer, of her ex-husband, Scottish*
comedian Jimmy Logan

The only real problem was thrashing out his contract. He told me he wanted his agent present – and in walked his Mum. I tell you this, she drives a hard bargain.
Allan McGraw, manager of Morton, after signing his son, Mark McGraw

British Rail stabbed us in the back by blowing the talks out of the water before they even got off the ground.
Jimmy Knapp, general secretary of the NUR

Despite what I'm about to say, I will not concede I'm a pessimist. Football has its head in the sand. We are part of the entertainment business.
Jim McLean, chairman of Dundee United

Our stock of commodes isn't a bottomless pit.
Argyll Health Board spokesman, begging patients given commodes on loan to return them, 1992

The propensity to truck, barter and exchange one thing for another . . . is common to all men, and to be found in no other race of animals.
Adam Smith

The trouble with employers is that they like ballots as long as you lose them.
Jimmy Knapp, June 1989

People are now discovering the price of insubordination and insurrection. And, boy, are we going to make it stick.
Sir Ian MacGregor, chairman of the National Coal Board (1983-6), during the miners' strike, 1985

Our business in this world is not to succeed, but to continue to fail, in good spirits.
Robert Louis Stevenson

CHANGE

Women aren't going to change anything until we get our trotters into the same troughs as they [men] do, in the same pens, in the same dirt.
Joan Burnie, *on International Women's Day, 1992*

Officials used to be anonymous but respected. Now it's the other way around.
Kenny Dalglish, *manager of Blackburn Rovers, 1995*

CHARACTER

Like most Celts, I'm moody.
Sean Connery, Sunday Express, *1967*

The crowd think he is posturing, call him 'big head'.
Arthur Rowe, *of Billy Bremner*, Encyclopedia of Association Football, *1960*

Souness was the tidiest man I've ever met. I'd throw my underpants in a corner, but he'd hang his on hangers.
Gordon Strachan, *footballer, of Graeme Souness,* Daily Record

Ian Fleming? A terrific snob, but very good company.
Sean Connery, Rolling Stone, *1981*

You can tell a good [football] player from a bad player simply by watching them run with the ball, on their own, with no one else in sight.
Jimmy Reid, *writer and columnist,* Daily Record, *1995*

If folk think I'm mean they'll no' expect too much.
Sir Harry Lauder *(1870-1950), music-hall entertainer*

As a politician, I loathed many of his policies. But I was interested in what had shaped him as a person.
Muriel Gray, *after interviewing Norman Tebbit*

Never heard tell of any clever man that came of
entirely stupid people.
Thomas Carlyle, *speaking in Edinburgh, 2 April 1886*

The King can be explosive and denunciatory, but
always with a twinkle in his eye.
John Buchan *(1875-1940), writer and statesmen, of
George V*

Let them cant about decorum
Who have characters to lose.
Robert Burns, *'The Jolly Beggars'*

I was born a Scotsman, and a bare one. Therefore
I was born to fight my way in the world.
Sir Walter Scott

I think for my part one half of the nation is mad –
and the other not very sound.
Tobias Smollett *(1721-71), novelist,* The Adventures of
Sir Lancelot Greaves, *1762*

Rangers like the big, strong, powerful fellows,
with a bit of strength and solidity in the tackle
rather than the frivolous, quick-moving stylists like
Jimmy Johnstone, small, tiptoe-through-the-tulips
type of player who excites the people.
Willie Waddell, *manager of Rangers, 1972*

He's got the heart of a caraway seed.
Bill Shankly, *referring to a player he had transferred*

I don't remember being shy. When other people
were shy, I used to ask why?
Winnie Ewing, *Scottish Nationalist politician, Scotsman,
1994*

I'm looking for Commander James Bond not an
overgrown stunt man.
Ian Fleming, *on meeting Sean Connery*

Some of my plays Peter out, and some Pan out.
J.M. Barrie, *author of* Peter Pan

CHAUVINISM

These skinny malinky long legs, big banana feet
have been held up in front of us for years now as
what women should be like locally, with their
washboard chests and wishbone legs.
Scottie McClue, *self-confessed male chauvinist, writer
and TV presenter*, Daily Record, 1995

That day of rest when New Women everywhere
were sitting feet up in their semmits, smoking their
pipes, not bothering to shave and watching the
Scottish Cup game on telly.
Tom Brown, *columnist, on International Women's Day*

Woman in her greatest perfection was made to
serve and obey man, not to rule and command
him.
John Knox, The First Blast of the Trumpet Against the
Monstrous Regiment of Women, 1558

Let me have my own way exactly in everything,
and a sunnier and pleasanter creature does not
exist.
Thomas Carlyle

I get great pleasure out of arranging flowers,
feminine little things I do around the house. I don't
go that mad, after all real blokes can only go so
far.
Rod Stewart, Daily Mail, 1993

Hawick is a very chauvinistic town but we can get
away with it as it's traditional.
Male participant in the town's Common Riding, Scotsman,
1994

I want someone to laugh with me, someone to be
grave with me, someone to please me and help my
discrimination with his or her own remark, and at
times, no doubt, to admire my acuteness and
penetration.
Robert Burns

CHILDREN

Parents learn a lot from their children about coping with life.
Muriel Spark, The Comforters

We have no qualms about taking on the landed gentry, no matter how exalted they are. They are all like spoilt children who won't share a toy.
Derek Keith, *Scottish campaign for public angling*, Scotsman, *September 1993*

The Scottish nation isn't ready to have our brood inflicted on them! There'd be nothing left up there.
Paula Yates, *TV presenter, revealing why she hadn't taken her daughter to Glasgow to visit her godfather,* Daily Record, *1993*

From his childhood this boy will be surrounded by sycophants and flatterers by the score, and will be taught to believe himself as of a superior creation.
Keir Hardie (1856-1915), *Labour politician, on the birth of the future King, Edward VIII*

The first thing I want to do is to see Eilish. I've missed her so much. When I've got her in my arms, that's when the celebrations can begin.
Liz McColgan, *Scottish athlete, first gold medallist at the World Championships in Tokyo, of her nine-month-old baby*

Men must learn that you can divorce your wife or dump your girlfriend . . . but you cannot do either to your children.
Joan Burnie

Men of her age are still able to have children naturally, yet there are no moves to stop them impregnating younger women.
Sheila MacLean, *professor of law and medical ethics at Glasgow University, responding to the furore over a 59-year-old woman who gave birth to twins, 1994*

Giving birth to Lola was the most wonderful moment of my life. She's everything I ever hoped for.
Annie Lennox, *singer*

CHOICES

Sixty's not so old is it? I put it in the same bracket as when your hair goes. Then you have only a couple of choices. When it's your age, you have no choice.
Sean Connery

If people have to choose between freedom and sandwiches, they will take sandwiches.
Lord Boyd Orr *(1880-1971), biologist, 1955*

Most things in excess are bad for us, including this current surfeit of food fascists, born-again non-smokers, and po-faced teetotallers. I would rather tread the primrose path with Rab C. Nesbitt, glass in my hand and cigarette too.
Joan Burnie

We may be in some degree whatever we choose.
James Boswell, *1712*

I considered that my native country afforded few opportunities of exercising my profession to any extent. I therefore judged it advisable (like many of my countrymen) to proceed southward, where industry might find more employment, and be better remunerated.
Thomas Telford *(1757-1834), civil engineer, of his decision to leave Scotland*

I'd rather lick stamps for a living than play for Hibs.
Brian Hamilton, *footballer, on joining Hearts,* Daily Record, *1995*

CLARET

Dr Johnson's absurdly crude view that claret is a wine for boys, with port allotted to men, was never shared in Scotland.
Ivor Brown, I Give You My Word, 1945

COMMUNICATION

All speech, written or spoken, is a dead language, until it finds a willing and prepared hearer.
Robert Louis Stevenson

In dinner talk it is perhaps allowable to fling any faggot rather than let the fire go out.
J.M. Barrie

If there are ladies present, I make sure there is nothing in my speech that I wouldn't want my own wife to hear.
Tommy Docherty, on after-dinner speaking engagements

Most parties in our time have the sense to recognise the Church's independence and to listen to what it says, whether it agrees or not.
Archbishop Winning, then Roman Catholic Archbishop of Glasgow, St Giles, 1993

Mr Watson, come here – I want you.
Alexander Graham Bell (1847-1922), scientist, the first words to travel by wire, Boston, 10 March 1876 (attrib.)

A little inaccuracy sometimes saves tons of explanation.
Saki (H.H. Munro), The Square Egg, 1924

Be not the slave of words.
Thomas Carlyle

They sacked me as nicely as they could. One of the nicest sackings I've had.
Tommy Docherty, on being sacked from Manchester United

Communism *v.* Alcoholism.
Scottish banner at the Soviet Union v. *Scotland World Cup match, 1982*

Don't worry, lads. Ally MacLeod's in Blackpool.
Scottish banner at World Cup match, 1982

I talk a lot on any subject. Which is always football.
Tommy Docherty

As I've said before and I've said in the past.
Kenny Dalglish

Let them specially put their demands in such a way that Great Britain could say that she supported both sides.
Ramsay MacDonald (1866-1937), *Prime Minister, referring to France and Germany*

They speak all the languages of the rainbow there.
Jackie Stewart, *world champion racing driver and commentator*

I always had a terrible fight to get work in Britain on account of my Edinburgh accent. And I still haven't lost it completely. I can't – I don't think it's right to lose it.
Sean Connery

CONFESSIONS

I'm a jambo and always will be.
Paul Smith, *Falkirk footballer and Hearts fanatic, 1992*

I'm a Hib at heart.
Alan Lawrence, *Airdrie footballer, admitting that even as a youngster he was a Hibs fan, 1992*

Even if I was an astronaut circling Mars, I'd still manage to go home for Christmas.
Lorraine Kelly

There is a fellow very like him [Henry, Lord Cockburn, the Solicitor General], who traverses the Pentlands in a dirty grey jacket, white hat, and long pole. That's not the Solicitor General, that's Cocky. And you may use all freedom with him.
Russell Hunter, *actor playing Lord Cockburn in the play* Cocky

There'll be a lump in my throat. But then there always is when 55,000 Scots sing our own national anthem.
David Sole, *Scotland Grand Slam skipper, making his last stand at Murrayfield, 1992*

I've seen too much of real life to be overawed by any pop stars with big egos.
Marlene Ross, *manager of rock group Runrig*

To make our idea of morality centre on forbidden acts is to defile the imagination and to introduce into our judgements of our fellow men a secret element of gusto.
Robert Louis Stevenson

As I don't know one end of a horse from another and have never been able to understand the fascination of the bad-tempered beasts, I might just take a rain-check.
Lorraine Kelly, *turning down an offer of riding lessons from an ex-show jumper*

CRICKET

Oh God, if there be cricket in heaven, let there also be rain.
Sir Alec Douglas-Home, *Conservative politician*

My wife had an uncle who could never walk down the nave of his abbey without wondering whether it would take a spin.
Sir Alec Douglas-Home, *BBC TV, 1982*

CRIME

We want what the public want – more police officers on the street, instead of the police being used as a political football.
James Fraser, *chairman of the Scottish Police Federation*

I think that if people were obedient to the Gospel, whatever puts murder in their hearts would not be there.
Revd Andrew MacLean, *convener of the Church of Scotland's Board of Social Responsibility, 1992*

Criminals have access to firearms on a scale never known to us before. They are proud of their weaponry, and the firearm has become a status symbol and a show of strength.
PC Tom Rowatt, *Strathclyde Police*

I'll bring back moves to bring back hanging.
Phil Gallie, *Conservative politician*

It's not a Scottish parliament that makes people scared to leave their homes at night; it is crime.
Tony Blair, *Labour politician, 1995*

Drink abuse plays a crucial part.
Father Tom Connolly, *Catholic leader, linking drink with crimes of violence*

Judges must have more powers.
Menzies Campbell, *Liberal Democrat politician, supporting harsher penalties for criminals, 1992*

Scots are living in fear and need help.
Henry McLeish, *Labour politician, advocating a review of policies in the light of an increase in violent crime*

CRITICISM

Thou eunuch of language; thou pimp of gender, murderous accoucheur of infant learning, thou pickled herring in the puppet show of nonsense.
Robert Burns, *to an anonymous critic*

His mind was a kind of extinct sulphur pit.
Thomas Carlyle, *of Napoleon III*

Poor Matt. He's gone to heaven, no doubt – but he won't like God.
Robert Louis Stevenson, *on Matthew Arnold*

McCoist is almost a one-off in Scotland.
Ivan Golac, *manager of Dundee United, suggesting that many Scottish players and managers take a negative approach to football and don't appear to enjoy the game*

People seem to be making a lot of the fact that I criticised my players after they had won. Surely that is as good a time as any to get things right.
Tommy McLean, *former manager of Motherwell, after beating Hearts and going top of the league, 1993*

When you look at the quality of the people who are doing the calling, you forgive.
Sir Ian MacGregor, *on the criticism he received during the miners' strike*, Daily Mail, *1984*

It is better to be thought of as a heart-throb than as a pig.
Tom Conti, *actor*

Oh, for an hour of Herod.
Anthony Hope, *theatre critic, at the opening of J.M. Barrie's* Peter Pan, *1904*

The ideal audience for this would be a house composed entirely of married couples who never had any children, or parents who have lost them all.
James Agate, *critic, of* Peter Pan

The criticism that Norman *Lament* made yesterday is frankly ludicrous.
Sir Norman Fowler, *of then Chancellor of the Exchequer Norman Lamont*

CUSTOM

Custom, then, is the great guide of human life.
David Hume, An Enquiry Concerning Human
Understanding, *1758*

Where beats the heart so kindly as beneath the
tartan plaid.
William Edmonstoune Aytoun *(1818-65), poet and
humorist, of Prince Charles Edward Stuart at Versailles,
1849*

A good breakfast, as usual in Scotland, with
findon haddocks, eggs, sweetmeats and honey.
Robert Southey, Journal of a Tour in Scotland in 1819

Unsuitable for a little Scot, I had to wear some
slimy green pants under my kilt.
Sir Nicholas Fairbairn

An English tea-party – you are offered a piece of
bread and butter that feels like a damp
handkerchief and sometimes, when cucumber is
added to it, like a wet one.
Sir Compton MacKenzie

The Western custom of one wife and hardly any
mistresses.
Saki (H.H. Munro), Reginald in Russia

I am not yet Scotchman enough to relish their
singed sheeps' heads and haggis . . .
Tobias Smollett

Fair fa' your honest, sonsie face,
Great chieftain o' the puddin' race!
Robert Burns, 'To a Haggis'

The Plaid itself gives pleasure to the sight,
To see how all its sets imbibe the light;
Forming some way, which even to me lies hid,
White, black, blue, yellow, purple, green, and red.
Allan Ramsay *(c.1685-1758), poet,* Tartana, *1718*

DANCE

For nought can cheer the heart so weel,
As can a canty Highland reel.
Robert Fergusson (1750-74), poet

My two worst dreads were dancing-class and
parties. Both caused me acute embarrassment.
Dancing was cissy and I had to wear my kilt,
which was then considered cissy too, although I
have worn it with pleasure ever since.
Sir Nicholas Fairbairn

For vivacity and agility in dancing, none excel the
Scotch ladies.
Edward Topham, 1776

DEATH

When my time comes, I want to die in bed,
listening to music and sampling a warming, well-
rounded 25-year-old. I mean whisky, of course.
Tom Brown, Daily Record

It is fitting that we should have buried the
unknown Prime Minister by the side of the
Unknown Soldier.
Lord Asquith (1852-1928), Liberal politician, of Andrew
Bonar Law, 1923

Here lies he who neither feared nor flattered any
flesh.
James Douglas, fourth Earl of Morton (c.1516-81),
Scottish courtier, at the burial of John Knox

For everyone who has been bereaved, giving up is
giving in and doesn't help.
Joan Burnie

For me it's more important when I'm going to die,
not how I'm going to die.
Sean Connery, after a health scare, El Pais, 1993

I believe sleep was never more welcome to a weary traveller than death was to her.
John Arbuthnot (1667-1735), *physician and writer, of Queen Anne*

Oh, Lord God, I have set my hope in thee!
My dear Jesus, set me free.
Mary Queen of Scots (1542-89), *shortly before her execution*

And though I think I would rather die elsewhere, yet in my heart of hearts I long to be buried among good Scots clods. I will say it fairly, it grows on me with every year; there are no stars so lovely as Edinburgh streetlamps.
Robert Louis Stevenson, The Silverado Squatters, *1883*

I'm heartbroken. He was like a father to all of us. He is among the great Scotsmen.
Winnie Ewing, *on the death of Donald Stewart, SNP politician, 1992*

He will be sorely missed. He was a fine Highland gentleman.
John Smith (1938-1994), *Labour politician, on the death of Donald Stewart*

Everything will be done in good taste.
David Hendry, *funeral arranger, announcing that his company would pioneer funeral advertising on Grampian Television, 1993*

Robin and Marian was supposed to be called 'The Death of Robin Hood', but Americans don't like heroes who die or anything that might smack of not being a victory.
Sean Connery, International Herald Tribune, *1983*

DESIRE

Women who wear short skirts are really tarts. They bleat about independence but they still want to be the object of men's desires.
Scottie McClue

I have a great desire to make people smile, not laugh. Laughter is too aggressive. People bare their teeth.
Muriel Spark, Times, 1983

I worry a lot more about sex than my career. I did want to be married by now. It must have been wishful thinking.
John Gordon-Sinclair, 1993

D R E A M S

Graeme Souness said he wanted me to help win titles and it has all come true.
Mo Johnston, footballer, after Rangers clinched the Premier Division Championship, 1991

I hope Scotland win the Rugby World Cup.
Dougie Donnelly, sports presenter, expressing his hopes for 1991

I hope for a peaceful winter in the hills.
Hamish McInnes, mountaineer and leader of Glencoe Rescue Team, 1991

Many's the long night I've dreamed of cheese – toasted, mostly.
Robert Louis Stevenson, Ben Gun, Treasure Island

D R E S S

There was no objection to the blue stocking, provided the petticoat came low enough.
Francis, Lord Jeffrey (1773-1850), critic and editor, of Mrs Hamilton, author of The Cottagers of Glenburnie, 1808

She just wore
Enough for modesty – no more.
Robert Buchanan, 'White Rose and Red'

Dress affects my feelings as irresistibly as music.
James Boswell, London Journal

He must be the worst-dressed man I have ever seen in my life.
Sharon Lovett, *fashion co-ordinator of* For Him, *of Rab C. Nesbitt*

They won't let us wear shorts because of the way they look. But if you'd seen how I looked as it was, you would know that doesn't make sense.
Sam Torrance, *golfer, suffering with perspiration whilst playing in the Johnny Walker Championship in Jamaica*

I usually match trousers, shirts and ties with casual jackets – but for dinners after internationals I wear a kilt.
Craig Chalmers, *rugby player*

I think I'm totally feminine. To me, real femininity is inside . . . It's not what you wear.
Sharleen Spiteri

Sir Alec is the first recorded case in history of a man who not only thinks he owns a Moss Bros. suit, but he owns Moss Bros. as well.
Harold Wilson, *Labour politician, of Sir Alec Douglas-Home*

DRINK

I don't drink because when I drank I used to hit people.
Billy Connolly, Sunday Times Magazine, 1994

Oh, aye, I used to drink an awful lot, but I don't do it anymore. I don't like hangovers
Frankie Miller, *singer, songwriter and actor, 1992*

It's not a disaster just a nuisance.
Stephen Crawley, *national sales manager, Caledonian Brewery, following a fire at the brewery,* Scotsman, *1993*

I couldn't let anyone come between me and my Kaliber.
Billy Connolly, *advertising Kaliber alcohol-free lager*

No drinking after 1 a.m.
John Temple, producer of Gaelic soap Machair, banning drink after one of the crew let a late-night bath overflow, 1992

George Best couldn't be here tonight. He was launching a ship in Belfast, and he wouldn't let go of the bottle.
Tommy Docherty, after-dinner speech

I'm a canny Scot and I like to make sure I'm getting value for money.
Jimmy Boyle, sculptor, writer and former criminal, of his interest in collecting good-value wine

I wasna fou, but just had plenty.
Robert Burns.

Your average British man likes to go and have a pint in the pub and enjoy it, and it's an intelligent man who can go there and know his limits.
Graeme Souness

The rituals of drink have always fascinated me. The way curry has become a sort of traditional Scottish food after a night of drinking.
Billy Connolly

Oh, thou demon Drink, thou fell destroyer;
Thou curse of society, and its greatest annoyer.
William McGonagall (1830-1902), poet, 'The Demon Drink'

To conduct it in the most rational and agreeable manner is one of the great arts of living.
James Boswell, on the pleasures of drinking

Beer does not taste like itself unless it is chasing a dram of neat whisky down the gullet, preferably two drams.
Sir Compton MacKenzie, Whisky Galore, 1907

I'll drink anything anybody gives me and enjoy it. I haven't stripped all the baggage of the past.
Jimmy Boyle, 1994

DRIVING

I hate the fact that women refuse to accept the fact that they are bad drivers.
Jim White, *television sports presenter, 1991*

Just as driving fast is dangerous, so is hogging country roads with ludicrous white hulks of tin that sit happily in front of a mile-long queue of cars.
Muriel Gray, *expressing her dislike of caravans, 1990*

DRUGS

It doesn't bother me as I am one of the cleanest sportsmen in the world. It just meant I had to drink a few more mineral waters.
Stephen Hendry, *speaking after his fifth random drugs test within a short period*, Daily Record

Make no mistake, Scottish football has its own coke-heads. It's common knowledge in drug-dealer circles that some players are using cocaine and other drugs as an alternative to alcohol.
Drugs counsellor and ex-addict

I am shocked. I have never heard of any footballer in Scotland getting up to anything like that.
Craig Levein, *captain of Hearts, of drug-taking among Scots footballers*

ECONOMICS

What we might call, by way of eminence, the dismal science.
Thomas Carlyle

It is the right product sold to a willing buyer that makes profit.
Sir Campbell Fraser, *chairman of Scottish Television plc*, Daily Telegraph, 1983

Making films can bring millions to the local economy, and Scotland is taking off as a film location.
Gordon Brown, Labour politician, at the Edinburgh Film Festival, 1992

Mr Major must face the fact that you cannot have a strong pound without a strong economy.
Robin Cook, Labour politician, 1992

Having added many millions to the natural riches, I therefore have a natural right to rest in my extreme old age.
James Watt

When I have to read economics documents, I have to have a box of matches and start moving them in position to illustrate and simplify the points to myself.
Sir Alec Douglas-Home

Our very integration in the British economy is both our greatest asset and the greatest flaw in the prospectus of Scottish separatists.
George Roberston

EDINBURGH

That knuckle-end of England.
Sydney Smith (1915-75), poet

Edinburgh is a cross between Copenhagen and Barcelona, except in Copenhagen they speak more understandable English.
John Malkovich, American actor, filming in Edinburgh, Scotsman, 1994

I wish you were in Edinboro' with me – it is quite lovely – bits of it.
Oscar Wilde (1854-1900), Irish playwright, novelist and poet, letter to E.W. Godwin, 17 December 1884

I think Edinburgh is a very flourishing city.
Margaret Thatcher, Conservative politician, giving a politician's answer when asked what she thought of Chancellor Lawson's budget, Independent, 1988

I've always been anxious among a lot of people whom I do not know, except in Edinburgh, where I have often been more uncomfortable among a lot of people whom I do know.
Sir Nicholas Fairbairn

This accursed, stinking, reeky mass of stones and lime and dung.
Thomas Carlyle, 1821

EDUCATION

His locked, letter'd braw brass collar,
Show'd him the gentleman and scholar.
Robert Burns, 'The Twa Dogs'

Good gracious, you've got to educate him first. You can't expect a boy to be vicious till he's been to a good school.
Saki (H.H. Munro)

At school, they said I had a high IQ, but I was useless at everything.
Midge Ure, rock musician

With a record like his, Michael Forsyth is lucky they've done away with the tawse.
Record Review, expressing a vote of no confidence for the then Education Minister's proposal to introduce performance league tables in schools, March 1992

To me, education is a leading out of what is already there in the pupil's soul.
Muriel Spark, The Prime of Miss Jean Brodie

It might have been teachers who gave us 'the tribe lives in mud huts and has rough mating on the floor'.
Dorothy Grace Elder, expressing the view that teachers as well as pupils are poor spellers, Scotland on Sunday, 1995

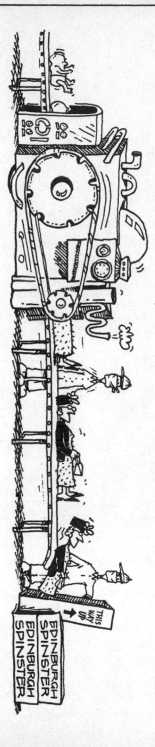

He patiently explained that the things called nets
were 'pockets', you 'potted' shots, not hit them,
and that a screw-shot wasn't an exotic cocktail.
Elsa McAlonan, *women's editor, trading places for
charity with snooker champion Stephen Hendry*, Daily
Record, *1992*

The General Strike has taught the working classes
more in four days than years of talking could have
done.
A.J. Balfour (1848-1930), *politician and philosopher*

Study most of all the strange cantrips of the
human heart.
Neil Munro (1864-1930), *novelist and journalist, 1926*

He was to Scotland what Martin Luther was to
Germany. 'Let the common people be taught' was
one of his messages.
Samuel Smiles (1812-1904), *writer and social reformer,
of John Knox*, Autobiography

As every Scot knows, a gallus besom is a cheeky
bitch.
Muriel Gray, *giving her interpretation of 'gallus besom'
after a London television company had translated it as a
'lively lass'*

The true University of these days is a Collection of
Books.
Thomas Carlyle, *1841*

Minds are like parachutes. They only function
when they are open.
Sir James Dewar (1842-1923), *physicist (attrib.)*

The Edinburgh Academy, from its birth, reflected a
degree of social or class orientation and . . . did
represent the first major break with the democratic
traditions of Scottish education.
Magnus Magnusson, *writer, broadcaster and TV
personality*, The Clacken and the Slate

We were kept about nine years at two dead
languages – Latin and Greek.
Henry, Lord Cockburn (1779-1854), *Solicitor General
for Scotland, describing his schooling in Edinburgh*

The beds are hard as iron, it's straw mattresses and bread and water. It's just like prison.
Prince Andrew, Duke of York, describing Gordonstoun School in Scotland, where he was a pupil

Those who become ministers in the House of Commons are those who do their homework.
Lord James Douglas-Hamilton, Scottish Office Minister, speaking in support of homework guidelines recommended by the Scottish Office, Scotsman, 1993

Our principal writers have nearly all been fortunate in escaping regular education.
Hugh MacDiarmid (Christopher Murray Grieve) (1892-1978), poet, Observer, 1953

I taught in a system that depended on the tawse, as we called the belt in Scotland.
A.S. Neill (1883-1973), educationist and founder of Summerhill School, which pioneered child-centred education and banned corporal punishment

Everybody has a degree in hindsight.
Wallace Mercer

EGOTISM

We can get wrinkles and it's attractive, women get them and they're over the hill.
Rod Stewart

Oh, I suppose I must have an ego to do this kind of thing, we all have I suppose.
Phyllis Logan, actress

I am a rogue at egotism myself; and, to be plain, I have rarely liked a man who was not.
Robert Louis Stevenson

Nothing Pam does surprises me any more.
Billy Connolly, of his wife, Pamela Stephenson, who climbed a ladder to muscle in on a celebrity photo session at Gleneagles, 1990

He is the daw with a peacock's tail of his own painting. He is the ass who has been at pains to cultivate the convincing roar of a lion.
T.W.H. Crosland, The Unspeakable Scot, *1902*

ENGLISH

We began to affect speaking a foreign language, which the English dialect is to us.
Alexander Carlyle *(1722-1805), divine and man of letters*, Autobiography, *1860*

Thirty millions, mostly fools.
Thomas Carlyle, *when asked the population of England*

ENTHUSIASM

Gie us an English heid.
Lou Macari, *of the atmosphere at England-Scotland games, epitomised by this chant, which made it difficult to play attractive football*

Love the show – didnae know opera had so many different stories.
Listener's remark to presenter Bill McCue of Radio Clyde on the show Who Disnae Like Opera?, *1993*

ENVIRONMENT

By the year 2020 we will have had to develop gills and will certainly have had to take some tips from Noah.
Dr John Harrison, *editor of Stirling University's climatological bulletin, predicting a dramatic increase in Scottish rainfall.*

VAT is not being applied to fuel because the Chancellor has gone green. It is being applied because the government's books have gone into the red.
Robin Cook, *1993*

Like charity, good environmental housekeeping
begins at home.
Gordon McDonald, *chairman of the Grampian
Economic Development Committee*, Scotsman, 1993

It consists of two things: stone and water. Like a
man in rags, the baked skin is still peeping out.
Dr Samuel Johnson (1709-84), *English writer and
critic, of the Scottish countryside*

EQUALITY

I believe in equality between the sexes – but I also
think that women should stick to things they are
good at. And reversing a car is not one of them.
Scottie McClue

They [women] are beginning to realise there are
things they can do, and we should let them.
Scottish male participant, on Channel 4 Men's Talk
programme, 1992

Equality of opportunity means equal opportunity
to be unequal.
Iain Macleod

As for International Women's Day: when there is
an International Men's Day, when some town
council holds an exhibition of Y-fronts, then – and
only then – will I participate.
Joan Burnie, 1992

Mr Liberal said he liked his wife to mother him.
Smother him would be more like it.
Kaye Adams, *presenter of* Men's Talk *programme,
Channel 4*

EXCUSES

Perhaps he was just annoyed because Liverpool didn't play very well.
Stephen Lodge, *referee, responding to comments made by Graeme Souness, then Liverpool manager, that the Southampton team were playing rough, 1992*

Let's forget jinxes or hoodoos. We lost before because we didn't play well enough.
Walter Smith, *rejecting the idea of a jinx on Rangers in the Scottish Cup, 1992*

I think it might be the damp of Glasgow.
Frankie Miller, *of his voice, which has been described as broken glass being dragged across sandpaper*

EXPERIENCE

They were magic. And ah'm glad they wis there fur tae haud me up.
Eric Cullen, *actor, at Glasgow Ice Show, featuring skating champions Torvill and Dean, 1992*

FAITH

They will prove they have the character and pride essential in this club.
Billy McNeill, *of Celtic, 1991*

Not exactly a very good advert for Lourdes is it? You go healthy and return a wreck.
Father Roddy MacNeill *of South Uist, whose group of Scots pilgrims fell ill on a trip to Lourdes, 1993*

She's the only woman in the world who has made me want to be faithful.
Rod Stewart, *of Britt Ekland*

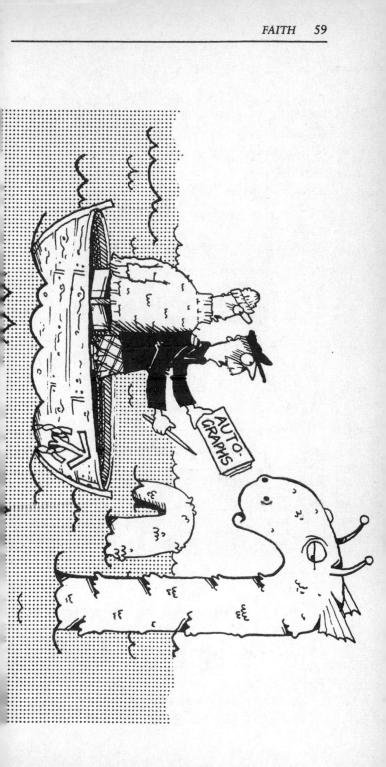

FAME

Fame is being asked to sign your autograph on the back of a cigarette packet.
Billy Connolly

Scotland's favourite redhead.
Ruth Wishart, *presenter of* Woman's Hour, *introducing actress Siobhan Redmond*

Look at that man's eyes. You will hear more of him later.
Andrew Bonar Law, *of Mussolini (attrib.)*

He had no ears for any charity unless labelled with his name. He would have given millions to Greece had she labelled the Parthenon 'Carnegopolis'.
Poultney Bigelow, *writer, of Andrew Carnegie,* Seventy Summers

A friend of mine once said to me, 'Everything is famous for something, and you are famous for living opposite Bernard Shaw.'
J.M. Barrie, *in his presidential address to the Society of Authors, 1928*

Tomorrow, every duchess in London will want to kiss me.
Ramsay MacDonald, *on forming the National Government*

FAMILY

The children used to kick my red boxes because they took up all my time.
Norman Lamont, *former Chancellor of the Exchequer, 1993*

I would never steal her limelight. I'd rather disappear into the heather.
Phyllida Law, *actress and mother of Emma Thompson, explaining why she rejects requests to appear on radio and TV chat shows since her daughter became the toast of Hollywood*

Now I see the talent he has, and I know he'll
become a better player than I ever was.
Allan McGraw, *manager of Morton, of his son, Mark, a*
Hibs striker, 1993

FAUX PAS

If I ever get pregnant, I shall be lying on the settee
with my feet up.
Lorraine Kelly

The Turkish Van, Abyssinian and British Blue are
all types of what ca . . . animal?
Magnus Magnusson, Mastermind *host*

When *Dr No* went to Japan, they translated it as
'No Need for Doctors'.
Sean Connery

Alex's story is not unusual – it is happening today,
in Scotland's capital city.
Caption in Edinburgh Evening News *alongside a*
photograph of Prince Charles in a feature on the homeless
headlined 'the Plight of the Lonely'

And tonight, *Coltrane in a Cadillac*, which is
basically Robbie Coltrane in an open-top Buick.
Simon Bates, *presenter, Radio 1, 1993*

With his great (and carefully calculated) talent for
putting his foot in it, we might consider Prince
Philip to be the most eloquent, literate and
classless member of the Royal Family.
Willie Hamilton, *anti-Royalist MP, 1982*

A toast . . . to Prince Charles and Lady Jane.
Peter Balfour, *chairman of the Scottish Council,*
proposing a toast to Charles and his bride-to-be (Diana),
1981

It was only a wee word. I covered it with a joke.
John Sessions, *after swearing during an interview on*
Radio 4

I thought you were dead.
A fan's comment to Scottish singer Lena Martell after she had been out of the limelight for several years

We welcome Robbie Coltrane's support for independence.
Alex Salmond, *SNP politician, responding to Robbie Coltrane's slip of the tongue at a Labour policy launch when he gave his support to independence*

I always get my fives and threes muddled up.
Norman Lamont, *former Chancellor of the Exchequer, who got his figures muddled while trying to explain why Britain needed to borrow £50 billion*

This is a rotten argument, but it should be good enough for their lordships on a hot summer afternoon.
A note on a ministerial brief read out by mistake in the House of Lords, Lord Hume, The Way the Wind Blows

One of Norman's problems is that he's terribly accident prone. If there's a banana skin around, he'll find it.
A friend of Norman Lamont, helping to clear up the controversy surrounding the former Chancellor's black eye

The paying customers who left early cheated themselves of exciting drama, despite the gusty wind.
Alex Cameron, *at Tynecastle, of fans who left before the end of a Hearts v. Celtic game*

Willie Lamont's relationship to that other Scots-born ball-dropper, the Chancellor, is unclear. Willie does, however, pronounce his second name properly, unlike Norman, who has gone all posh since leaving his native Shetland and now insists on putting the emphasis on the 'ont'.
Alistair Campbell, *on why Cowdenbeath Football Club are doing badly – their goalkeeper is called Lamont*

I think he's a great player.
Kenny Dalglish, *on being asked his thoughts on Brazil during the 1982 World Cup*

Many a man who thinks to found a home discovers that he has merely opened a tavern for his friends.
Norman Douglas, South Wind, *1917*

FEAR

There is an element creeping in of the antagonism which is found at football matches, which didn't used to exist, and is a source of genuine concern.
Bill McLaren, *rugby commentator, of the atmosphere at Five Nations Championship matches, 1995*

These are crypto-scare tactics. Major's beleaguered government is rattling the cage and dreaming up bogeys.
Andrew Jaspan, *editor of* The Scotsman, *following John Major's attack on Labour proposals for a Scottish Assembly,* Guardian, *1994*

We had to stand in line, and right in front of me was this big fat girl with great big arms. Her arm was directly at my eye-level. They stuck her with the hypodermic needle, and I saw the whole thing.
Sean Connery, *explaining his dislike of needles, 1992*

I was wondering what part of me he'd eat first.
David Livingstone, *describing how he felt when being savaged by a lion*

I just had to find the woman inside of me, which in a way was quite scary.
Peter Capaldi, *of his role as a drag artist in a TV drama, 1993*

I'm so frightened. I got the water wings on and a rubber ring around my middle. That's fine – but when I take all these things off I go down like a stone.
Annette Cosbie, *on learning to swim, 1993*

Today, ours is a fearful, anxious, nail-biting nation ruminating on Burns' salutation to human despair: An' forward tho' I canna see, I guess and fear.'
Jim Sillars, *SNP politician,* The Case for Optimism

I have never been nervous in all my life, and I have no patience with people who are. If you know what you're going to do, you have no reason to be nervous.
Mary Garden, *Scottish opera singer (1847-1967), when asked if she ever felt nervous during a performance*

FILMS

A film set is a never-ending hell.
Tom Conti, *1983*

FISHING

Fishing is undoubtedly a form of madness but, happily for the once-bitten, there is no cure.
Alec Douglas-Home

The charm of fishing is that it is the pursuit of what is elusive but obtainable, a perpetual series of occasions for hope.
John Buchan, New York Times, *1951*

FOOD

I'd sooner starve.
Julia Roberts, *American actress, when asked if she would eat haggis, June 1994*

My lords and lieges, let us all to dinner, for the cockie leekie is a-cooling.
Sir Walter Scott, The Fortunes of Nigel, *1822*

FOOTBALL

It was the blackest day of my life.
Denis Law, *footballer, referring to the 1968 European Cup final, which he missed through injury*

What distinguishes Scottish soccer, perhaps, is the permanent triumph of hope over experience.
Clifford Hanley, *writer, 1980*

All this talk about Tommy Docherty not being fit to run a football club is rubbish. That's exactly what he's fit for.
Clive James, *1979*

Football is so unpredictable, you can't say it's all over bar the shouting.
Joe Jordan

The team have lacked resilience, organisation and determination. If Joe can bring us these things, we'll be back.
Liam Brady, *speaking of the management partnership between himself and Joe Jordan at Celtic*, Scotsman

Some people think football is a matter of life and death . . . I can assure them it is much more serious than that.
Bill Shankly, Sunday Times, *1981*

Johnny Methold has been wonderful. He's done everything on the ground tonight.
Ian St John, *commentator, during a Spurs v. Feyenoord game*

The best thing in football is scoring goals – and I'm a top scorer.
Ally McCoist, *Rangers footballer*

. . . Association Football is becoming notorious for scenes and disgraceful exhibitions of ruffianism . . . the rabble will soon make it impossible for law-abiding citizens to attend matches.
Scottish Athletic Journal, *1887*

On my first day as Scottish manager I had to call off practice after half an hour, because nobody could get the ball off wee Jimmy Johnstone.
Tommy Docherty, *1970*

This would bring a tear to a glass eye.
Jimmy Nicholl, manager of Raith Rovers, after his First
Division side defeated Celtic on penalties to lift the Scottish
Coca-Cola Cup, 1994

While everyone is worrying about passes, he can
run with the ball.
Walter Smith, manager of Rangers, of Danish star Brian
Laudrup, Edinburgh Evening News, 1994

. . . And the football it has robbed him o' the wee
bit sense he had.
Jimmy McGregor, singer-songwriter, 1960

Half a million for Remi Moses? You could get the
original Moses and the tablets for that price!
Tommy Docherty, 1982

Kenny Dalglish has about as much personality as a
tennis racquet.
Mike Channon, English footballer

He can't run, he can't tackle and he can't head the
ball. The only time he goes forward is to toss the
coin.
Tommy Docherty, of Ray Wilkins

If Everton were playing at the bottom of my
garden, I'd draw the curtains.
Bill Shankly

Ally McLeod believes that tactics are a new kind
of peppermint.
Anon.

FOOTBALL BLOOMERS

The advantage of being at home is very much with
the home side.
Denis Law

. . . but the ball was going all the way, right away,
eventually.
Archie MacPherson, commentator

You cannot guarantee a thing in this game. All you can guarantee is disappointment.
Graeme Souness

Not being in the Rumbelows Cup for those teams won't mean a row of beans, 'cos that's only small potatoes.
Ian St John

Ferguson was signed not for the present but for the future.
David Murray, *of Duncan Ferguson, who was sold to Everton early in the next season*

That's the kind he normally knocks in in his sleep – with his eyes closed.
Archie MacPherson

Without picking out anyone in particular, I thought Mark Wright was tremendous.
Graeme Sounness, *football commentary*

FOOTBALL FANS

We do have the greatest fans in the world but I've never seen a fan score a goal.
Jock Stein *(1922-85), Scotland team manager, during the World Cup in Spain, 1982*

Come along the Rangers
Buckle up your belts
You'll mebbe beat the Hearts
But you'll never beat the Celts.
Celtic song

Follow, follow, we will follow Rangers
We arra people.
Rangers fans call-response chant

Their [football fans'] ability to smuggle drink into matches makes Papillon look like a learner.
Scottish Police Federation spokesman, *1981*

Rangers are a big-time club, but their fans are not big time.
Alex Ferguson, upset by booing during a pre-season tournament at Ibrox, Daily Record, *1994*

What they [fans] want to see is the ball being centred and their team making a beeline for that bloody goal.
Alex Ferguson

The world and FIFA acknowledge Scots fans are the best behaved, but the BBC is trying to lower them to the level of the English thugs.
Chris McLean, expressing disapproval that Scots fans are lumped in with others when violence is reported at football games, 1990

FUN

I am one of those who always think it fun to be in Scotland.
Hilaire Belloc (1870-1953), French-born British writer and poet, Places, *1942*

The tackling might be fun.
Clare Grogan, whose fantasy on Trading Places Swap Shop, *a television progranne in aid of charity, was to be a Celtic footballer, 1992*

I'm not upset about it. You've got to be a sport if something like this happens to you.
Carol Smillie, television presenter, victim of a hoax on a popular show, 1993

There are far too many people in the game who are unhappy. Football is a business – but fun must come first.
Ivan Golac

FUTURE

I intend to be around for a long time, so there are plenty more goals to come.
Ally McCoist

The passion of prying into futurity makes a striking part of the history of human nature.
Robert Burns

There will be fewer clubs. I believe there will be a maximum of two leagues, with 12 teams in each.
David Murray, *predicting the shape of football in the year 2015, 1993*

I think it would be fair to say that Formula One has been lulled into a sense of complacency in recent years but after this weekend it is going to have to take a very long, hard, careful look at safety, and very quickly.
Jackie Stewart, *racing driver, calling for better safety standards and a boycott of dangerous race tracks*

The status quo has been left far behind as a credible option.
Alex Salmond, *during discussions on a Scottish Assembly*

Nuclear war lies, if it lies anywhere, in the future.
Ludovic Kennedy, *broadcaster and writer*

GALLUS

If Muriel Gray started to show off as a child, her dad would call her a gallus little besom.
Beverly Morrison, *writer*

As every Scots knows, a gallus besom is a cheeky bitch.
Muriel Gray, *correcting a London television company which had translated 'gallus besom' as 'lively lass'*

It's a very street word and we mean it in the most modern sense. It means to be cool. Benny Lynch personified that. He came from a humble background yet he conquered the world.
Mark Rankin, of pop band Gun, on why they feature Benny Lynch on the cover of their album, Gallus, 1992

Gallus – an instantly available Scottish word, still used, and meaning 'deserving the gallows'.
W. Gordon Smith, writer

It's a blend that's a hit with all ages, from gyrating teenagers to gallus grannies.
James McBeth, writer, of Runrig

GENEROSITY

And I don't mind sharing the award with David Mellor as long as he doesn't expect me to suck his toes.
Rab C. Nesbitt (Gregor Fisher), accepting the Least Sexy Celebrity Award

GENIUS

Och, just let him on the park.
Jock Stein, when asked whether footballer Kenny Dalglish's best position was in attack or midfield

As our regular listeners will know, Christmas has come and gone.
Douglas Cameron

The crash of the whole solar and stellar systems could only kill you once.
Thomas Carlyle, letter to John Carlyle, 1831

Denis was in the class of Di Stefano, because he could do everything: organise a side and score goals. His close control was not as good perhaps, but he beat people by his speed of thought.
Harry Gregg, Manchester United goalkeeper, of Denis Law

The Lisbon Lions were a better all-round team,
and we had one player of genius they don't have,
Jimmy Johnstone.
Tommy Gemmell, *footballer, reflecting on the state of*
Scottish football, 1993

A genius of a player . . . a credit to the game on
and off the pitch.
Tommy Docherty, *of Kenny Dalglish*

He was born with a great gift.
George Best, *footballer, of Kenny Dalglish*

If a poll were to be conducted among my
contemporaries as to who was the greatest Scottish
player they ever saw, the outcome would be Jim
Baxter.
Alan Sharp, *novelist and film-maker, 1976*

GLASGOW

He has not the brains of a Glasgow baillie.
Lord Asquith, *of Andrew Bonar Law, 1916*

There's no better place to do that than Glasgow.
Graeme Kelly, *guitarist with Deacon Blue, justifying*
using scenes of Glasgow as a backdrop for their video,
1989

It's great to get back to reality once in a while.
Jonothon Malone, *beauty stylist, returning to his home*
town of Glasgow, Daily Record, *1993*

Glasgow . . . the vomit of a cataleptic
commercialism.
James Leslie Mitchell (Lewis Grassic Gibbon)
(1901-35), novelist, The Thirteenth Disciple, *1931*

Glasgow now means nothing to the rest of Britain
but unemployment, drunkenness and out-of-date
radical militancy.
Alasdair Gray, *novelist, 1982*

But the great thing about the way Glasgow is now is that if there's a nuclear attack it'll look exactly the same afterwards.
Billy Connolly, Gullible's Travels, *1982*

Probably about two or three hundred pounds a week.
Stuart Kennedy, former Rangers goalkeeper, when asked the biggest difference between playing for Forfar and Rangers

I've been all over the world, and you can't get anything near the people of Glasgow – they're friendly and very real.
Frankie Miller, 1992

The misty smoke and the tenements of Glasgow, caught in the light, made a magic of their own.
Guy McCrone (1898-1977), novelist, The Philistines, *1947*

O Glasgow famed for ilka thing
That heart can wish or silver bring.
John Mayne (1759-1836), poet, 'Glasgow', 1783

G O B B L E D Y G O O K

At the risk of sounding too hippy dippy, the songs on this album were conceived in a more organic way.
James Grant, singer with Love and Money, 1993

His tables pay no regard to the catchment areas of the schools. They disregard unemployment and poverty.
Dr John Reid, MP for Motherwell North, expressing his concern at the government's proposals to introduce performance league tables in schools, 1992

Are you really arguing to me that there will be a serious body of opinion in the EC that will want to exclude from membership the country with 70 to 80 per cent of the EC's oil and gas reserve?
Alex Salmond, to Brian Walden

It used to make me mad to read some of the piffle written about the English set-up, but now I just have a good belly laugh to myself . . . it is so much nonsense.
Danny McGrain, *Celtic and Scotland captain, of biased football reporting, 1978*

I thought I had a good understanding with Basile Boli. He didn't understand me and I didn't understand him.
Alan McLaren, *footballer, after making his debut for Rangers*

There's enough Ferraris there to eat a plate of spaghetti.
Jackie Stewart

Les Dawson offers his congratulations on the birth of the baby and, after all, he should know. He drove tanks in Korea.
Selina Scott, *television presenter*

He will cause problems in the air, and the changes he could create from that are really meat and drink for Ally McCoist.
Simon Stainrod, *manager of Dundee, of Mark Hateley, 1992*

A pass rising a yard above the ground should be a foul: a player receiving a pass has two feet and only one head.
William Read, *manager of St Mirren, before the Scottish Cup final, 1959*

It was a very physical fight.
Jim Watt, *former boxer and sports commentator, of the fight between Roberto Duran and Ken Buchanan*

G O L F

Golf is a thoroughly national game, it is as Scotch as haggis, cockie-leekie, high cheekbones, or rowanberry jam.
Andrew Lang *(1844-1912), journalist and essayist,* Lost Leaders, *1889*

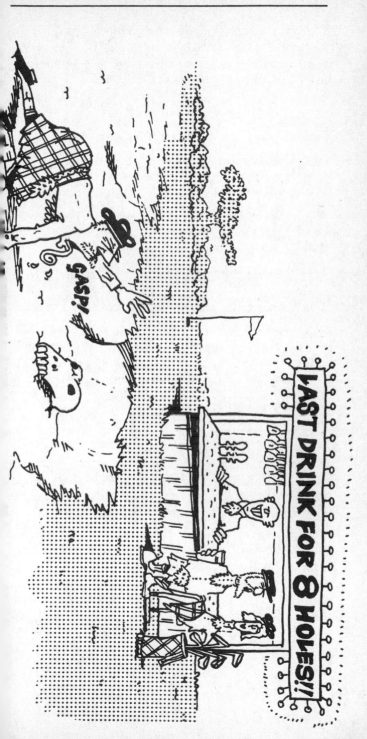

During nearly 200 years from the Peace of
Glasgow in 1502 to the Revolution of 1688, every
reigning monarch of the Stuart line was a golfer.
Robert Browning, History of Golf, 1955

I am cracking up through having too many
weekends off.
Sandy Lyle, golfer, questioning his fitness, 1993

All I've got against it is that it takes you so far
from the clubhouse.
Eric Linklater, referring to golf

Pinero has missed the putt – I wonder what he's
thinking in Spanish.
Renton Laidlaw, journalist and golf commentator

He is a wonderfully gifted golfer, but he needs to
lighten up.
David Feherty, golfer, of Colin Montgomerie

It's a great thrill and a real honour. As a good
patriot, I hope a few Scots play their way into my
team.
George MacGregor, Walker Cup captain, on his
appointment

The game of golf is an intensely Presbyterian
activity.
Clifford Hanley

So he goes from three under to three over, all in
one foul sweep.
Renton Laidlaw

Of this diversion the Scots are so fond, that when
the weather will permit, you may see a multitude
of all ranks from the Senator of Justice to the
lowest tradesman mingled together in their shirts,
and following the ball with the utmost eagerness.
Tobias Smollett, 1771

HAPPINESS

If there be such a thing as true happiness on earth, I enjoy it.
Tobias Smollett, The Adventures of Roderick Random, *1748*

They don't realise that in Glasgow there is no such word as 'happy'. The nearest we have is 'giro' or 'blootered'.
Rab C. Nesbitt (Gregor Fisher)

There is no duty we so much underrate as the duty of being happy.
Robert Louis Stevenson

I am very happy with my life but I *do* hope someone will make flights leave on time.
Jim Watt, *1991*

Alana is tall, Alana is blonde. For the first time in my life, I found it was possible to be happy with a flat-chested woman.
Rod Stewart, *of his first wife, Alana Hamilton*

A society can surely be flourishing and happy, of which the far greater part of the members are poor and miserable.
Adam Smith, *Scottish philosopher,* An Inquiry into the Nature and the Causes of The Wealth of Nations, *1776*

I'm calmer these days and it's a great relief. This new record is certainly not as bloody miserable as a lot of the stuff I've done before.
Annie Lennox, *singer,* Independent Magazine, *1992*

Celtic will be glad to be sitting in the bath now with two points tucked under their belt.
John Greig, *sports commentator*

Come, let me know what it is that makes a Scotchman happy!
Samuel Johnson, *calling for a gill of whisky, in Boswell's* Journal of a tour to the Hebrides, *1773*

If people are happy they'll give 110 per cent.
Jimmy Gordon, *managing director of Radio Clyde,*
giving his recipe for good staff morale, 1993

I've never at any time had withdrawal symptoms
from my retirement. I have never had an itch to
get back in.
Jackie Stewart

HATRED

The thing I hate about women is that they are
normally right.
Billy McNeill, *manager of Celtic*

Smoking is the one thing I really can't take. I can't
bear it.
Paul Coia, *television presenter, describing his pet hate,*
1991

I am deeply uncomfortable being Chancellor with
this level of borrowing. I hate it.
Norman Lamont, *interviewed by the* Guardian
newspaper on the morning of his sacking, Independent,
1993

Where on that day a dreary gloom appears
And the kirk bells ring doleful in your ears.
James Boswell, *expressing his dislike of Sundays in*
Edinburgh

Her tactics are ridiculous. She was so close, I was
tripping up and having to keep checking back –
she knows it annoys me.
Liz McColgan, *10,000 metres world champion runner,*
expressing annoyance at her rival Yvonne Murray's tactics,
BUPA International Festival of Running, 1993

I certainly didn't do it deliberately. It's inevitable
that there will be a bit of bumping on a course
with tight bends like that.
Yvonne Murray, *after winning the 5,000 metre race*
against Liz McColgan, 1993

I hate, loathe and detest, mannish women.
John Cairney, actor

I put comfort before appearance. I couldn't bear to
live in something that looked like a show house.
Lorraine Kelly

Hatred; Hatred is by far the longest pleasure
Men love in haste, but detest in leisure.
Lord Byron

I hated school. I got distracted too easily.
Midge Ure

Fie on the life of this world! Speak not to me of it
any more.
Queen Margaret of Scotland (1424-44), *who was
married at the age of 12 to Dauphin Louis XI, who
despised her*

HEROES

With his clothing and his cars and his wines and
his women, Bond is a kind of present-day survival
kit. Men would like to imitate him – or, at least,
his success – and women are excited by him.
Sean Connery, Playboy, 1965

Ten times the player Keegan was.
Denis Law, *of Kenny Dalglish*

I could follow him around the world in my shift.
Mary Queen of Scots, *of James Hepburn – Earl of
Bothwell*

Football has probably lost the greatest ambassador
it has ever known. No matter what era he had
been manager, he would have been the greatest.
Denis Law, *of Sir Matt Busby, 1994*

We see her [Skye athlete Karen McLeod] as a
symbol which will give an incentive for other
young people. It is always important to have
heroes.
Donnie Munro, Scotsman, 1995

Scot Liz McColgan is one of Britain's true sporting heroes. And people like Frank Bruno, Gazza and English rugby and football teams are nothing but second-rate flops.
Chris Eubank, *boxer*

Rod Stewart, because he's your ultimate lad. He's someone people can relate to, and he's launched 100 bad haircuts among disc jockeys.
Terry Christian, *television presenter, naming the guest he would most like to interview*

HISTORY

Now there's ane end of ane old song.
James Ogilvy, *Earl of Seafield (1664-1730), as he signed the Act of Union, 706*

The quick life of today sounding among the relics of antiquity, and over-shadowed by the august traditions of a Kingdom, makes residence in Edinburgh more impressive than in any other British city.
Alexander Smith, *1865*

The most notorious whore in the world.
Peter Wentworth, *writer, of Mary Queen of Scots*

HONESTY

You blew it.
Jimmy Bone, *manager of Airdrie, to his team, after they missed a penalty and dropped a vital point*

If the team has played badly and you think the manager will give you a rollicking, you won't be disappointed by Graeme Souness.
Ray Wilkins, *former Rangers footballer*

Victor is a Rolls Royce moving like a Mini.
Jim McLean, *expressing concern over the fitness of Argentinian footballer Victor Ferreyra of Dundee United*

Yes, I am smug. People say I'm smug. It's true. But I'm smug and honest.
Alex Salmond, *1995*

HONOURS

I am proud to accept this honour in recognition of John's contribution to the Labour Party and to British political life.
Elizabeth Smith, *wife of the late Labour leader John Smith, after being awarded a life peerage in the New Year Honours List, 1995*

Sir James Watt? Never.
James Watt, *on being offered a baronetcy*

This caps a tremendous year for me.
Gavin Hastings, *on receiving the OBE in the New Year Honours List, 1993*

Everyone said it was a great honour, but for me the last reason on earth to accept something like this is because you consider it an honour.
Donnie Munro, *accepting rectorship of Edinburgh University*

I just can't envisage Margaret Herbison from Shotts being a baroness.
Margaret Herbison, *Labour politician, receiving the honour and explaining why she would not take her place in the House of Lords, 1993*

It's a great honour to be given this dizzy by the 17-year-old lassies of Britain.
Rab C. Nesbitt (Gregor Fisher), *accepting the Least Sexy Celebrity Award, 1992*

It doesn't matter much. I'll still get treated with the same abuse at home.
Magnus Magnusson, *on receiving his honorary knighthood, 1988*

HUMOUR

Ron Atkinson couldn't make it. His hairdresser died . . . in 1946.
Tommy Docherty, *after-dinner speech*

It requires a surgical operation to get a joke well into a Scotch understanding.
Sydney Smith

He uses statistics as a drunken man uses lamp-posts – for support rather than illumination.
Andrew Lang

I sometimes think that when the Prime Minister tries to select a weapon it is the boomerang he finds most effective.
John Smith, *of John Major,* Observer, *1993*

2 beautiful Highland Bollocks, 1 blond, 1 red, ideal attraction around Hotels and Parks, delivery can be arranged. Offers over £325 each.
Tony Troon, The Best of the Scotsman Diary

Unlike Kaliber, it doesn't make you fart.
Billy Connolly, *comparing advertising Kaliber alcohol-free lager with the Rover Metro car, 1989*

Do you think it pleases a man when he looks into a woman's eyes and sees a reflection of the British Museum Reading-Room?
Muriel Spark

All the poison that my honourable friend suggested I would happily take, rather than be spreadeagled on the floor of the house by her.
Nicholas Fairbairn, *in a retort to Edwina Currie during the 'fluoridation' debate in the House of Commons*

One is pleased to have amused Sir Alastair.
Rab C. Nesbitt (Gregor Fisher), *on hearing that Sir Alastair Burnet, television newsreader, had turned up to his retirement leaving party at ITN wearing one of Rab's vests*

Willie [Ormond] never gave us talks about foreign teams, because he couldn't pronounce their names. But once in Scandinavia he stopped us as we were going out and said, 'Watch out for the big blond at corners, and free kicks.' So we went out onto the field and looked across at them, and there were about six big blonds. Well, we were playing Sweden!
Scottish player, 1974

The world population must be amused – is it to be the football field, or the dram shop?
Scottish Athletic Journal, *1883*

Take me to Largs – I'm for a cappucino at Nardini's right now.
Robbie Coltrane, adding levity during filming A Tour of the Western Isles, *1993. Nardini's café on Scotland's west coast is renowned for its coffee and cakes*

David Steel was shot dead outside his house in front of his wife and child. The date was 20 December 1686. Doubtless there have been times when some wished that his descendant might suffer the same fate.
David Steel, Against Goliath

Salman Rushdie phones to say, 'Wallace, you are bad news. I don't want anything to do with you.'
Wallace Mercer, when, as Hearts chairman, he attempted to take over Hibernian, 1990

George Bush has said that humour will be dominating his re-election campaign. What's his evidence? A second-hand joke about Bill Clinton as the Karaoke Kid.
Gordon Brown, Labour politician

The day I'm no longer funny is when I'll give up.
Ricki Fulton, comedian

IDENTIFICATION

Scotland and Ireland are more important than Hollywood.
Emma Thompson, just before the 1993 Hollywood Oscar ceremony

I am the man in the street.
Sir Arthur Conan Doyle

There is no way Ryan Giggs is another George Best. He is another Ryan Giggs.
Denis Law

Being British is a faith. I'll never lose it.
Sir Ian MacGregor, Sunday Times, 1986

Indeed, I come from Scotland, but I cannot help it.
James Boswell, on being introduced to Dr Samuel Johnson

I am not Mrs Branagh. I am, and always will be, Emma Thompson.
Emma Thompson

INERTIA

When a man hasn't a good reason for doing a thing, he has a good reason for letting it alone.
Sir Walter Scott

Extreme busyness, whether at school or college, kirk or market, is a symptom of deficient vitality.
Robert Louis Stevenson, An Apology for Idlers

A bunch of lazy gits.
John Lambie, manager of Partick Thistle, describing his players after a defeat against Rangers, Daily Record, 1995

INVENTION

The artist cannot attain to mastery in his art unless he is endowed in the highest degree with the faculty of invention.
Charles Rennie Mackintosh, *'Seemliness', 1902*

'The Baird Undersock'
Medicated, Absorbent and Soft, keeping feet warm in winter, cool in summer. Ninepence per pair. Post free.
John Logie Baird *(1888-1946), electrical engineer and television pioneer, advertising an early invention in a local newspaper*

KNOWLEDGE

We are slowly realising that any knowledge to improve the human mind should be communicated to women no less than men.
History of the Burgh and Parish Schools of Scotland, 1876

I'm not saying that the Ministry of Defence in London does not have the whole picture of what is going on, but they only have a partial one.
Sir David Steel, *commenting on the Gulf War*

The charge he must answer is not that he ever arranged with the noble lords to meet around the back of a motorway service station to pick up his bung and hand over the gong. The charge is much more urbane. Word gets around that the chances of a peerage or knighthood are multiplied by generous donations.
Robin Cook, *addressing Sir Norman Fowler in the Commons, recommending that all party funding should be public knowledge, 1992*

I gained much general knowledge, and when I went to medical school I had a great advantage over my fellow students, who were straight from school and had never got away from their books into the school of life.
Sir Alexander Fleming (1881-1955), bacteriologist and the discoverer of penicillin, who worked as a clerk before going to medical school

Knowledge is power and I've got a lot to learn. But I believe I can win races. and if you win races, you win championships.
David Coulthard, racing driver, 1995

Madness need not be all breakdown, It may also be breakthrough.
R.D. Laing (1927-89), psychiatrist.

LAW

Consider what you think justice requires, and decide accordingly, but never give your reasons; for your judgement will probably be right, but your reasons will certainly be wrong.
William Murray, first Lord Mansfield (1705-93), lawyer and politician, advice to a newly appointed colonial governor, The Lives of the Chief Justices of England, *1849*

Do you not speak English? If you think aye in Scots means yes, it doesn't.
Sheriff Irvine Smith, Scotsman, 1994

A statesman is judged by results. If his policy fails he goes. It may be unfair, but there is a kind of rough justice about it.
Baron Robert Boothby (1900-86), Conservative politician

LEADERS

You can't lead your troops if you are a little man with a white face who is so frightened he can't even express himself.
Ivan Golac, expressing his views on the state of Scottish football, 1995

A born leader of men is somebody who is afraid to go anywhere by himself.
Clifford Hanley

LIFE

Such accidents will happen in the best regulated families.
Christopher North (1785-1854), critic and essayist, Blackwood's Magazine, *1830*

My life was spent in one long effort to escape from the commonplace of existence.
Sherlock Holmes, in 'The Red Headed League', by Sir Arthur Conan Doyle

It seems to be quite in vogue now.
Siobhan Redmond, of her role in a television drama as a lesbian, 1995

For one man that can stand prosperity, there are a hundred that will stand adversity.
Thomas Carlyle

There are two problems in my life. The political ones are insoluble and the economic ones are incomprehensible.
Alec Douglas-Home, 1964

To get anywhere in life you have to be anti-social. Otherwise you'll end up being devoured.
Sean Connery, Sunday Express, *1967*

Society goes on and on and on. It is the same with ideas.
Ramsay MacDonald, 1935

He appeared honourably ineligible for the struggle
of life.
Cyril Connolly *(1903-74), English writer and journalist,*
of Alex Douglas-Home

LIFESTYLE

I might have a swmming-pool and, of course, a
golf course; but apart from that I'm quite easy to
please.
Sean Connery, *stating some of his requirements when*
househunting in Beverly Hills

This'll make a few people a bit sick but I don't
usually get up till 8.30.
Ally McCoist, Sunday Times, *1993*

I'm not a big spender. I do carry cash, although my
wife will probably deny it.
Norman Lamont, Sunday Times, *1993*

It's as intrusive as a nightmare.
Sean Connery, *of playing James Bond, 1971*

LOTTERY

People of 16 can engage in what may be the
biggest lottery in life by getting married. Why on
earth should they not be allowed to buy lottery
tickets?
John Maxton, *Labour politician*

Even having four winning numbers in the lottery
didn't cheer me up.
Brian Hamilton, *describing his feelings after leaving*
Hibernian on a matter of principle, Daily Record, *1995*

Kennedy in his suit tailored for King Kong was the
real prize.
John Gibson, *columnist, of actor Gordon Kennedy who*
represented Scotland in the National Lottery draw,
Edinburgh Evening News, *1995*

LOVE

It is very rarely that a man loves
And when he does it is nearly always fatal.
Hugh MacDiarmid (Christopher Murray Grieve)
'The International Brigade'

I trusted and loved him, and he had affairs.
Britt Ekland, of her relationship with Rod Stewart,
Evening Standard, 1994

If they only married when they fell in love, most
people would die unwed.
Robert Louis Stevenson

Better lo'ed ye canne be,
Will ye no come back again?
Caroline Nairne (1766-1845), songwriter, referring to
Bonnie Prince Charlie, from the song 'Charlie is my
Darling'

My love she's but a lassie yet.
James Hogg (1770-1835), poet and writer, song title

Music has given me everything I've got. At the
moment, I'm not going to give it up for anything.
Sharleen Spiteri

If they have only a loving heart, willing hands and
common sense, they will not need fine English, for
there is none to admire it . . .
Mary Slessor (1848-1915), missionary, on the
qualifications needed for helpers in her missionary work in
Africa

But to see her was to love her,
Love but her, and love for ever.
Robert Burns, 'Ae Fond Kiss'

I'm desperately serious.
Rod Stewart, of Joanna Lumley

I love all women, modern and non-modern alike.
Pat Lally, head of Glasgow City Council

The sweet post-prandial cigar.
Robert Buchanan, 1874

How delicious is the winning of a kiss at love's beginning.
Thomas Campbell (1777-1844), *poet and journalist*

Man's love is of man's life a thing apart, 'tis woman's whole existence.
Lord Byron

Let no one who loves be called altogether unhappy.
Even love unreturned has its rainbow.
J.M. Barrie, The Little Minister

To be overtopped in anything else I can bear; but in the tests of generous love I defy all mankind.
Robert Burns, *letter to Clarinda*

Better to be courted then jilted
Than never be courted at all.
Thomas Campbell, 'The Jilted Nymph'

L O V E R S

I have been punished for falling in love. What I have done is nothing at all to do with my track record as a manager.
Tommy Docherty, *following his sacking by Manchester United for 'breach of contract' after admitting an affair with the wife of the club's physiotherapist, 1977*

This idea that Scottish men are unromantic and that Europeans are the best lovers – that's complete rubbish. Scottish men are right up there in the passion league.
Jane Davidson, *lingerie party organiser, who organises lingerie-buying parties for businessmen, 1993*

LUCK

I don't have good-luck charms but I do hate changing my boots. And I'll always follow Stuart McCall out of the tunnel, which is a bit ridiculous, but I'll always do it.
Ally McCoist

Personally, I think if a woman hasn't met the right man by the time she's 24, she may be lucky.
Deborah Kerr, *Scottish-born American actress*

He's a lucky b******. But he'll go through life like that and there's no point in me trying to change him.
Walter Smith, *of Ally McCoist, who came on as a substitute and scored the winning goal in the League Cup final, 1993*

LYING

Oh what a tangled web we weave
When first we practise to deceive!
Sir Walter Scott

If we don't make it, I'll go bungee jumping without the rope.
Matt Hall, *chairman of Gala Fairydean, in advance of his club's ultimately unsuccessful bid for election to the Scottish League, 1994*

The cruellest lies are often told in silence.
Robert Louis Stevenson

MAN

A man's a man for a' that.
Robert Burns

A man willing to work, and unable to find work, is perhaps the saddest sight that fortune's inequality exhibits under the sun.
Thomas Carlyle, Chartism, *1839*

The world is neither Scottish, English, nor Irish, neither French, Dutch, nor Chinese, but human.
James Grant (1822-87), *novelist and historian, on founding the National Association for the Vindication of Scottish Rights, 1852*

No great man lives in vain. The history of the world is but the biography of great men.
Thomas Carlyle

Men are never so good or so bad as their opinions.
Sir James Mackintosh (1765-1832), *philosopher and historian,* Dissertation on the Progress of Ethical Philosophy, *1830*

It is impossible to persuade a man who does not disagree, but smiles.
Muriel Spark, 1962

Men are nervous of remarkable women.
J.M. Barrie, What Every Woman Knows, *1908*

I call them weekend wimps. Usually they only take an active part when, after being prodded with a French loaf, they surrender their wallet at the checkout.
Jim Blair, journalist, in a feature on men and shopping, Daily Record, *1990*

Man's the oak, woman's the ivy.
J.M. Barrie, What Every Woman Knows, *1908*

They are men, not machines.
David Murray, acknowledging that fewer games for the top clubs will help his team to succeed in Europe, 1994

The mystic bond of brotherhood makes all men one.
Thomas Carlyle

Man is a creature who lives not upon bread alone, but principally by catchwords.
Robert Louis Stevenson

If I am a great man, then a good many of the great men of history are frauds.
Andrew Bonar Law

Every man at the bottom of his heart believes that he is a born detective.
John Buchan

MAN AND WOMAN

The little rift between the sexes is astonishingly widened by simply teaching one set of catchwords to the girls and another to the boys.
Robert Louis Stevenson

I prefer the straightforwardness of men.
Sharleen Spiteri, admitting she is a tomboy, Record Woman, 1993

They are the biggest bunch of nerds this side of a lager-louts' convention, boasting about their sex lives.
Joan Burnie, of a survey of men's attitudes towards sex, 1992

MARRIAGE

I've been married six months. She looks like a million dollars, but she only knows 120 words and she's only got two ideas in her head. The other one's hats.
Eric Linklater, Juan in America

Once you are married, there is nothing for you, not even suicide, but to be good.
Robert Louis Stevenson

I wouldn't want to marry anyone else.
Rod Stewart, of girlfriend Dee Harrington

Complete innocence, especially in matters matrimonial, is a fairly rare flower.
Joan Burnie

I rather think of having a career of my own.
A.J. Balfour, when asked if he would marry Margot Tennant

The two women I've married have both been high
profile, so you could say I like a challenge . . . But,
in fact, you get no choice: you fall in love, and
that's that.
Jim Kerr, 1995

It's sweet surprises like that which keep our
marriage alive.
Rab C. Nesbitt (Gregor Fisher), *after his wife clubbed
him over the head for coming home drunk*

Marriage is one long conversation, chequered by
disputes.
Robert Louis Stevenson

Marriage is a wonderful invention, but then again
so is a bicycle-repair kit.
Billy Connolly

Brides look so pretty on their wedding day. They
are often not pretty at other times, but they are all
pretty on their wedding day.
J.M. Barrie

Billy and Pamela wore Versace as well. Matching
like a lavatory and its chain. Very tasteful and in
tune with the occasion.
Joan Burnie, *of Billy Connolly and his wife Pamela
Stephenson at the wedding of singer Sting, 1992*

In a marriage a man becomes slack and selfish,
and undergoes a fatty degeneration of his moral
being.
Robert Louis Stevenson

MEDIA

The *Scotsman Newspaper* has been published! It is
flourishing in a vigorous manhood, immeasurably
the best newspaper that exists or has existed in
Scotland.
Lord Cockburn, *on the first publication of the* Scotsman,
1817

It is heartening that there is such interest in the broadcasting industry and the contribution it makes to Scotland.
John McCormick, *controller of BBC Scotland, during the campaign for greater autonomy in Scottish broadcasting, 1993*

I very much regret the loss of Alastair Campbell, a journalist held in the highest regard in his profession, from the political editorship of the *Daily Mirror*.
John Smith, Today, 1993

I cringe when I look back on my first appearances.
Ian St John

A man who spent the last eight years working with Franciscan monks punched a woman and hit another when they refused to kiss him on the Edinburgh-Glasgow train.
Glasgow Evening Times

What a piece of advertising this is to get. We'll be in on the most watched sporting event in the world.
Peter McLean, *Celtic public relations official, after Celtic had secured pitch-side advertising at the World Cup final*

We have some ten per cent of the population but this is not reflected in the programmes we put out. Talent disappears down south.
Muriel Gray, *referring to BBC Scotland,* Herald, 1993

It will be noticed that in all the islands there are a great number of illiterates . . . English to them is unreadable.
Scotsman, 1886

I don't think any broadcaster could resist the chance to be involved in the start of something new.
Jimmy Mack, *disc jockey, on leaving BBC Scotland for Radio Clyde, 1989*

I have long ago learned that the only true things in the newspapers are the advertisements.
Norman Lamont, *on reports that he would stand against John Major*, Quote Unquote, *1994*

Christianity, of course, but why journalism?
A.J. Balfour, *in reply to the statement 'all the faults of the age come from Christianity and journalism'*, Margot Asquith, *Autobiography*

You have a great future in televison.
Producer of A Kick in the Ballots, *of Charles Kennedy, Liberal politician who chairs the quiz programme*, Sunday Times, *1993*

The *Guardian* will realise that the *Observer* is a turkey.
Andrew Neil, *former editor of the* Sunday Times, *writer and broadcaster*, Guardian, *1994*

As a model democratic party for all of our 60 years, there has never been, and never will be, a place for anti-English sentiment in the ranks of the SNP.
Alex Salmond, Scotsman

MEMORIES

This is *it*, I'm going to be a great rugby player. I took it out on boxing day and lost it in the bushes.
Paul Coia, *on being given a rugby ball when a young boy*

My memories of the Motor Show go back to when my father had the garage in Dumbuck.
Jackie Stewart, *on opening the Scottish Motor Show*

I remember him telling the Commons that one constituent claimed to be in communication with the spirit of Robert Burns – and Burns had reported his hatred of the Poll Tax.
Gordon Brown, *of George Younger, former Scottish Secretary*, Daily Record

They were tough times, but then it was tough for everyone. If you wanted a new pair of shoes, you went to the baths on a Saturday night.
Tommy Docherty, *remembering his childhood*

He was a good friend and a true gentleman. I played against him many times for Scotland, it was always a challenge.
Denis Law, *of Bobby Moore*

The sight of Bobby Moore holding the trophy aloft just rubbed salt into the wound.
John Greig, *remembering watching Bobby Moore hold up the World Cup in 1966, a competition for which Scotland had not qualified*

He was one of the best defenders I have ever seen. He was also a very nice man.
Alex Ferguson, *paying tribute to Bobby Moore*, Sunday Times, *1993*

Preston? They're one of my old clubs. But then most of them are. I've had more clubs than Jack Nicklaus.
Tommy Docherty, *1979*

I cannot remember if I saw the 1966 final but I am quite clear in my mind about what I thought of Bobby. His middle name should have been 'class', in capital letters.
Andy Roxburgh, *former Scotland team manager, tribute to Bobby Moore*

God gave us our memories so that we might have roses in December.
J.M. Barrie

MODESTY

Scots are so used to being a provincial backwater that we shy clear of making claims about our potential impact upon the wider human scene. But it is time to set aside this self-effacement.
Jim Sillars, Scotland – A Case for Optimism, *1985*

I don't feel such a big fish. I understand that my
name has a certain power. I know that people will
answer my calls – but I don't use any of that
much.
Annie Lennox, Independent Magazine, 1992

I can be better than I was in 1991. I have
absolutely nothing to prove to anyone other than
myself.
Liz McColgan, runner, of her comeback after injury
before competing in the London Marathon, Mail on
Sunday, 1995

There was no objection to the blue stocking,
provided the petticoat came low enough.
Francis Lord Jeffrey, of Mrs Hamilton, author of The
Cottagers of Glenburnie, 1808

I can't see the likeness myself – I'm far better
looking.
James Macpherson, actor, admitting fans have mistaken
him for fellow Scottish actor John Leslie

I honestly thought Woody Allen would have
beaten me to it.
Rab C. Nesbitt (Gregor Fisher), on receiving an
award for the Least Sexy Celebrity, 1992

MONEY

Whenever I think about the budgetary problems, I
think of Errol Flynn . . . reconciling net income
with gross habits.
Malcolm Rifkind, Conservative politician

No complaint is more common than that of a
scarcity of money.
Adam Smith, An Inquiry into the Nature and Causes of
the Wealth of Nations

It's not as easy as it used to be to make a buck.
Gordon McDonald, Grampian councillor, on the
region's economic fortunes, 1995

We sailors get money like horses and spend it like asses.
Tobias Smollett

The game's no longer the thing, but the size of the cheques.
Joan Burnie, *of the changing face of sport*

The real truth is that most clubs, at all levels, are either bust or close to it. They are a bank manager's nightmare.
Alex Cameron, *sports columnist,* Daily Record

MORALITY

Here lies the bones of Elizabeth Charlotte,
Born a virgin, died a harlot.
She was aye a virgin at seventeen,
A remarkable thing in Aberdeen.
Anon.

If your morals make you dreary, depend on it they are wrong.
Robert Louis Stevenson

MUSIC

I knew more about Geordies then than I did about Gaels, and I found it quite extraordinary – all these wee lassies singing the same song and things like that, many of them unable to speak Gaelic, having just learned the songs phonetically. I couldn't make head nor tail of it.
Alistair Moffat, *television presenter, on making a film about the Mod, his first task on joining Scottish Television, 1982*

History in rock'n'roll terms is three minutes long and ends on a major chord.
Ian Macdonald, *BBC Radio Scotland*

The theme tune from *The Archers*.
Billy Connolly, *on being asked to suggest a suitable alternative to the National Anthem*

I didn't mind playing second or third fiddle in the orchestra. What I will say, though, is that the orchestra must have a new conductor.
Wallace Mercer, *on standing down as chairman of Hearts*

You may remember this music from the film *10* when Bo Derek said it was her favourite music to make love to.
Carl Davis, *conductor, conducting the Royal Scottish Orchestra, and introducing Ravel's* Boléro *to the audience*

I warned you, Carl, never to mention sex in Glasgow.
Chief Executive of the Royal Scottish Orchestra, replying to Carl Davis

When a strange group from Scotland comes to town, you have to be good to impress anyone.
Texas, *on hitting New York, 1989*

Choral competitions have done more harm to Gaelic than any over-fishing has done to the Minch.
Black Angus, *poet*

I thought they were wonderful – they were so incredibly different.
Alistair Moffat, *on discovering the Scottish group Runrig*

I lost all my friends in the Bay City Rollers disaster of 1974, it was like some plague, a complete wipe-out . . . from the moronic prancing and chanting, from their gormless uniformed pools-winner faces, from their tartan trimmings and short pants.
Julie Burchill, *journalist and author*, The Face, 1984

There is a case for Wet, Wet, Wet at the Baker Street lost-property office.
Laura Lee Davies, Time Out

He was probably born to be chairman of Watford
Football Club, and now he's beginning to look like
the chairman of Watford Football Club.
Rod Stewart, *of Elton John, 1977*

Rod should stick to grave-digging 'cos that's where
he belongs, six feet under.
Elton John, *in reply to Rod Stewart, 1977*

Karaoke Kinnock, the man who'll sing any song
you want him to.
Ian Lang, *Conservative politician, of Neil Kinnock, 1992*

The only trouble is this collection of divine
melodies leaves an absolute blank on the brain . . .
like afternoon Radio 2. The sort of music that
won't disturb your grandmother.
Claire Sheaff, *critic, of Scots singer Sheena Easton's
album* The Best Kept Secret, *Rolling Stone*

NATION

None can destroy Scotland, save Scotland itself . . .
My Lord, patricide is a greater crime than
parricide.
Lord Belhaven, *opposing the Act of Union of 1707*

When it comes to Scotland, you'll not shut me up.
I am entitled to be involved, I have a birthright in
Scotland.
Sean Connery, *responding to politicians who attacked
his support for the Scottish National Party, 1991*

Our real enemies are among us, born without
imagination.
R.B. Cunninghame Graham *(1852-1936), author and
politician, of the enemies of Scottish Nationalism, in a
speech at Bannockburn, 1930*

NEW MAN

I do everything except breast-feeding.
Andy Gray, *comedy actor, of his contribution to shared parenthood*

NICKNAMES

Ormond, to many senior players was too nice a man to be a successful international manager . . . Donny Osmond was one of the nicknames he was given.
Danny McGrain

NOTORIETY

Burke's the butcher, Hare's the thief,
Knox the boy who buys the beef.
Contemporary jingle, of the body snatchers, Burke and Hare, c. 1820

NUDITY

For many people, nudism may be totally off-putting and increase stress levels.
Prem Misra, *psychiatrist, responding to the Council for British Naturism who advise stripping off to relieve stress, 1992*

ODDBALLS

If some women want to get all hot and bothered chasing balls, who am I to object?
Joan Burnie, *of Monica Seles, tennis player, 1990*

If an entire nation can be kicked in the crotch, the last swing of Jon Callard's boot had that effect at Murrayfield.
Hugh McIlvanney, *sportswriter, of the last-minute penalty goal scored by Jonathan Callard, which enabled England to beat Scotland at Murrayfield*

Margaret Thatcher has chickened out – or, to quote her own terminology, she is 'a frit'.
Dennis Canavan, *Labour politician on Margaret Thatcher's decision not to give evidence before a Commons committee inquiring into the Malaysian dam project*, Quote Unquote

Anyone who buys into all that celebrity lifestyle stuff can't quite understand your motivation – or lack of it. They think you're weird, Howard Hughes-ian.
Jim Kerr, *admitting that he prefers privacy to publicity*

When I see pictures of myself on stage dressed up in bizarre outfits and women's clothes, I think to myself, my god, I look like a big bloody lorry driver in drag.
Andy Bell, *singer*

That really seemed like the Gobi desert there – not a red shirt anywhere.
Bill McLaren, *during a Scotland v England rugby game*

Glasgay, this arty-farty festival for homosexuals, is beyond a joke. It is a total and complete waste.
Joan Burnie, *protesting against the Glasgow Gay Festival, 1993*

The most frightening fact about AIDS is that it can be spread by normal sex between men and women. This is still rare in Scotland.
Scottish Sunday Mail

There is a great peculiarity about the Highlands and Highlanders; and they are such a chivalrous, fine, active people.
Queen Victoria *(1819-1901)*

OLD AGE

I couldn't retire.
Sean Connery, Film Yearbook, *1985*

OPINION

They had hardly any trade, any money, or any elegance.
Dr Samuel Johnson, *of the Scots*

I believe sleep was never more welcome to a weary traveller than death was to her.
John Arbuthnot, *of Queen Anne*

That was so silly. I don't think viewers want to see short skirts or me grinning all the time.
Lorraine Kelly, *following the departure of presenter Fiona Armstrong on GMTV, who was told to smile and show off her legs to play on the 'F (Fanciability) Factor'*

Every so often Britain turns out a good film – that doesn't mean a comeback. I know they say it is – for a whole two weeks! America makes films all the time and suddenly Britain thinks it's going to corner the world market in movies – it's fanciful nonsense.
Tom Conti, *1983*

Ian Fleming? A terrific snob, but very good company.
Sean Connery, Rolling Stone, *1981*

Very innocent girls are usually very stupid girls.
Sir Compton Mackenzie, Sinister Street, *1913*

Opinion polls are about as scientific as looking at the entrails of a chicken.
Jim Sillars, *1992*

Lots of times, managers have to be cheats and conmen. We are the biggest hypocrites. We cheat. The only way to survive is by cheating.
Tommy Docherty, *1979*

What do you think of English football? Again, the answer is simple: 'Not bloody much'.
Danny McGrain, 1978

I have no patience whatever with these gorilla damnifications of humanity.
Thomas Carlyle, on Darwin's The Origin of Species

London is a splendid place to live for those who can get out of it.
Lord Balfour

Everything that is most beautiful in Britain has always been in private hands.
Malcolm Rifkind, Observer, 1988

A people whose modest but confident boast is that they always let the horse go before shutting the stable door.
James Cameron, of the English, What a Way to Run a Tribe, 1963

I'm glad she's gone from Downing Street. She didn't care.
Peggy Herbison, of Margaret Thatcher

OPTIMISM

We were bombarded with crap about beating the rest of the world into the ground. How could anyone be so optimistic about our chances?
Lou Macari, when a member of the Scotland team under manager Ally Macleod, Argentina, 1978

This morning's policy launch made it clear that we will have a Labour government this year and a Scottish Parliament next year.
Robbie Coltrane, referring mistakenly to independence at the Labour Party's devolution policy launch, 1992

He is leaving behind the Old Firm goldfish bowl.
Andy Goram, of Duncan Ferguson, Edinburgh Evening News

We've only had three rude signs so far this time.
Winnie Ewing, on the campaign trail, Scotsman, 1993

PATRIOTISM

I may speak with an English accent but there's never been any doubt about which country I wanted to represent.
Scot Gemmill, *Nottingham Forest footballer and son of former Scotland skipper Archie Gemmill, 1992*

The country must have one clan, as it were – a united people working in co-operation and co-operatively using the wealth it has created.
John MacLean, A Hail! The Scottish Communist Republic

Our real enemies are among us, born without imagination.
R.B. Cunninghame Graham, *speaking out against the enemies of Scottish Nationalism, Bannockburn, 1930*

Scotland means everything to me.
Frankie Miller, *1992*

After illicit love and flaring drunkenness, nothing appeals so much to Scotch sentiment as having been born in the gutter.
T.W.H. Crosland

I don't brandish it like a flag or anything, but my upbringing is important to me.
Phyllis Logan, *of her Scottish childhood*, Sunday Mail, *1994*

Gentlemen, from my infancy to this moment I have devoted myself to the cause of the people. It is a good cause – it shall ultimately prevail – it shall finally triumph.
Thomas Muir (1765-99), *advocate and campaigner for parliamentary reform, speech at his trial, 1793*

This is a fight to end government of Scotland by England for England, from England.
Ian Hamilton, *SNP candidate for the European Parliament, adoption speech, 1993*

I detect a sense of rampant nationalism attracting people along to watch international games, where there is not so much a desire as a need to win.
Bill McLaren, *of international rugby matches*

I think of myself as 99.9 per cent Scottish.
David Jackson, *adopted Peruvian son of Scots surgeon Ian Jackson, who rebuilt his face*, Daily Record, 1993

For as long as but ane hundred of us remain alive, never will we on any conditions be brought under English rule. It is in truth not for glory, nor riches, nor honours that we are fighting, but for freedom – for that alone, which no honest man gives up but with life itself.
Declaration of Arbroath, 1320

PHILOSOPHY

Be a philosopher, but amidst all your philosophy, be still a man.
David Hume

In my end is my beginning.
Mary, Queen of Scots (1542-87), *after her capture by the English, 1568*

I wanted him to be the kind of man who had never walked along the beach and felt the grass under his feet.
Bill Forsyth, *film director, of a character in one of his films*

Thou are not alone, if thou have faith.
Thomas Carlyle

I'm a people's man, a player's man. You could call me a humanist.
Bill Shankly, *1976*

If you can't fail, you can't do anything, and it was brilliant advice.
Emma Thompson, *recalling advice given to her by her father*

I don't compromise beliefs – and I don't suffer
fools gladly.
Muriel Gray

He is a professional and a gentleman but
unfortunately personalities have to be put aside
when you are talking about survival.
Donnie MacIntyre, *chairman of Ayr United Football
Club, after sacking the manager,* Sunday Mail, *1993*

PLACES

Stirling, like a huge brooch, clasps Highland and
Lowlands together
Alexander Smith, *'A Summer in Skye', 1865*

I would rather go back to Africa than practise
again in Peebles.
Mungo Park, *quoted by John Buchan in his foreword to*
Leaves from the Life of a Country Doctor

A sink of atrocity, which no moral flushing seems
capable of cleansing.
Lord Cockburn, *of Dundee,* Circuit Journeys, *1888*

And ye'll ken richt well
by the afa' smell
the next stop's Kirkcaldy.
Sir David Steel, *quoting doggerel referring to the train
journey from Edinburgh to his home town, Kirkcaldy*

They have not even the implements of cleanliness
in this country.
Tobias Smollett, Travels through France and Italy, *1766*

I am very glad to have seen the Caledonian Canal,
but don't want to see it again.
Matthew Arnold (1822-88), *poet and critic, letter to his
wife, 1882*

PLEASURE

There is nothing – absolutely nothing – half so much worth doing as messing about in boats.
Kenneth Grahame (1859-1932), writer, The Wind in the Willows, *1908*

Nine years ago, when half an hour into the New Year I fell in love with the man I'm married to.
Liz Lochhead, poet, writer and actress, remembering her best year, Guardian, *1994*

I found a party with a young and vigorous outlook and I thought that I could work with them.
Ian Hamilton, QC, on re-joining the SNP

For several days after my first book was published I carried it about in my pocket, and took surreptitious peeps at it to make sure the ink had not faded.
J.M. Barrie

I play every game as if it was my last. That's why I enjoy it so much.
Mark Hateley, Rangers footballer

POETRY

A poet without love were a physical and metaphysical impossibility.
Thomas Carlyle

Poetry was always my first love.
Iain Cuthbertson, actor

Poets . . . though liars by profession, always endeavour to give an air of truth to their fictions.
David Hume, 1739

I'd heard of a man named Burns – supposed to be
a poet;
But, if he was, how come I didn't know it?
They told me his work was very, very neat,
So I replied: 'But who did he ever beat?'
Muhammad Ali, *boxer, on his visit to Burns country,*
1965

POLITICAL GIFTS

Some well-known Scots were asked to suggest gifts
for John Major on his fiftieth birthday:

A miner's lamp as a memento of a once great
industry.
Tom Clarke, *shadow Scottish Secretary*

A map of Scotland so he knows where we are.
Margaret Ewing, *parliamentary group leader of the*
Scottish National Party

A bottle of Scottish water that's not for sale.
Henry McLeish, *shadow Scottish Industry Minister*

A layman's guide to the European Common
Fisheries Policy.
Bob Allan, *chief executive of the Scottish Fisherman's*
Federation

Enough money to pay his Maastricht bill so he
and Alex Salmond can stop double-dealing.
Tommy Brennan, *former convener of shop stewards at*
Ravenscraig

Redundancy – the same as our members are
facing.
Brian Negus, *chairman of the Industrial Trades Unions*
at Rosyth

The gift of charisma and caring and a copy of the
constitution for a devolved Scottish Parliament.
Jim Devine, *Scottish regional officer with COSHE*

A basic state retirement pension, asking him to
survive on it given the increases in VAT on fuel.
Jim Wallace, *leader of the Scottish Liberal Democrats*

A new stocktaking ledger engraved as follows:
'11 out of 72 is not a mandate'.
Campbell Christie, STUC general secretary

POLITICS

We all know that prime ministers are wedded to
the truth, but like other wedded couples they
sometimes live apart.
Saki (H.H. Munro)

All I say is, if you cannot ride two horses you have
no right to be in the circus.
James Maxton (1885-1946), politician, on being told
that he could not be in two political parties, Daily Herald,
1932

If we are to have clear and sound thinking, the
people must take politics very seriously and be
very well informed about them.
John Buchan, address on 'Literature and Life', 1910

Among the foot-soldiers of the SNP these days,
Alex Salmond is about as popular as Flodden.
Angus Macleod, columnist, referring to SNP leader Alex
Salmond leading his fellow SNP MPs Margaret Ewing and
Andrew Welsh into the voting lobby with the Tories on
Maastricht, Mail on Sunday, 1993

Everything Alex said about Paddy Ashdown voting
with Tories can be thrown back in his face. The
fact that he does not bother consulting the grass-
roots will come back to haunt him.
SNP member

I am often asked if non-political people talk to me
about Maastricht. The answer is yes – the most
common question is: when will this bloody
Maastricht thing finish?
George Robertson

All political parties die at last of swallowing with
their own lies.
John Arbuthnot

Politics have always been my chief interest.
John Buchan, *to Stanley Baldwin, 1932*

Politics is perhaps the only profession for which no preparation is thought necessary.
Robert Louis Stevenson

John Major thinks this man is a serious political figure.
Alastair Campbell, *of Jeffrey Archer,* Sunday Mirror, *1992*

She has done for our party what King Herod did for babysitting.
Andrew MacKay, *of Edwina Currie*

All politicians have vanity. Some wear it more gently than others.
Sir David Steel, 1985

END THE FORSYTH SAGA
SNP banner, referring to Michael Forsyth, the Conservative Scottish Office Minister, 1992

COMING SOON: FORSYTH III
Banner in support of Michael Forsyth

May I suggest he pursue his alternative career and conducts orchestras since he does not know how to conduct himself.
Nicholas Fairbairn, *of Edward Heath*

The heterosexual wing of the Labour Party.
George Foulkes, *Labour politician of the Social Democratic Party (SDP)*

Old politicians never die, they simply wade away.
Malcolm Rifkind, *of John Stonehouse MP, who was involved in a fake drowning incident*

He's like Fagin – 'You gotta pick a pocket or two' – the battle hymn of any aspiring Labour Chancellor.
Michael Heseltine, *of John Smith, Labour politician, 1992*

I have never thought of myself as a Scottish nationalist, but in the few months that I have been in this house I have been rapidly coming to the conclusion that the only solution is a Scottish government.
John Robertson, *speech in the House of Commons, 1961*

I thought he was a young man of promise; but it appears he was a young man of promises.
A.J. Balfour, *of Winston Churchill on his entry into politics, 1899*

Go back to your constituencies and prepare for government.
Sir David Steel, *speech to party conference, 1985*

He is used to dealing with estate workers. I cannot see how anyone can say he is out of touch.
Lady Caroline Douglas-Home, *daughter of Alec Douglas-Home, when asked about her father's suitability for his new role as Prime Minister,* Daily Herald, *1963*

Being Chancellor of the Exchequer is a humdrum activity.
Norman Lamont, Mail on Sunday, *1991*

No Chancellor until this one has come to the House and said that because he has money available to him the rich will get the benefits and the poor will make the sacrifices.
Gordon Brown, *of Nigel Lawson's budget speech,* Observer, *1988*

He has not the brains of a Glasgow baillie.
Lord Asquith, *of Andrew Bonar Law, 1916*

It is fitting that we should have buried the unknown Prime Minister by the side of the Unknown Soldier.
Lord Asquith, *1923*

Bonar would never make up his mind on anything. Once a question had been decided, Bonar would stick to it and fight for it to the finish, but he would never help in the taking of a decision.
David Lloyd-George *(1863-1945), Liberal politician*

Every time the Labour Party are asked to name their weapon they pick boomerangs.
Ian MacLeod

He created the impression of being rather dated, rather fuddy-duddy, rather aristocratic, indifferent in health and altogether too well-mannered for politics in the age of Harold Wilson.
Sir Gerald Nabarro, *of Alec Douglas-Home, 1963*

We have heard of people being thrown to the wolves, but never before have we heard of a man being thrown to the wolves with a bargain on the part of the wolves that they would not eat him.
Andrew Bonar Law, *referring to the fact that the then War Minister, Col. Seely, had offered his resignation, 1914*

The party that likes to leave us gasping: that's the new Labour. John Smith is the caring, comfy and safe figure that the electorate wants – but at heart he is a corporatist.
Alastair Burnet, *journalist,* Sunday Times, *1993*

POSTERITY

We will surely write the script for the next generation with this.
Jackie Stewart, *backing a new race circuit near Edinburgh*

PRAISE

The Big Bow-Wow strain I can do myself like any now going; but the exquisite touch, which renders ordinary commonplace things and characters interesting, from the truth of the description and the sentiment, is denied to me.
Sir Walter Scott, *in praise of Jane Austen, journal, 1826*

A good book is the purest essence of a human soul.
Thomas Carlyle, *speaking in support of the London Library*

Kane is that rare breed . . . a pop singer with a brain.
Billy Sloan, music critic, of singer Pat Kane's performance on the television programme Open to Question

He's a very sharp guy and a great writer.
Douglas Vipond, of Deacon Blue, of William McIlvanney, who wrote lyrics for the group, Daily Record, 1989

That young lady has a talent for describing the involvements and feelings and character of ordinary life which is to me the most wonderful thing I ever met with.
Sir Walter Scott, of Jane Austen, journal, 1826

They call him Saint Nick – let's say he's very caring and compassionate.
Linda Campbell, wife of radio and television presenter Nicky Campbell

If Davie Cooper had been playing in the Olympics he would have been drugs tested.
Iain Campbell, in praise of Motherwell footballer David Cooper, 1992

Genius (which means transcendent capacity of taking trouble, first of all).
Thomas Carlyle, of Frederick the Great

John, you're immortal.
Bill Shankly, to Jock Stein in the Celtic dressing-room after the European Cup final victory over Inter Milan, 1967

If he was a chocolate drop, he'd eat himself.
Archie Gemmill, of his team-mate Graeme Souness, 1978

I think we sound brilliant on this album.
Pat Kane, of Hue & Cry, 1993

To Wendy Wood whose friendship I have enjoyed for 35 years, and who, throughout those years, has never failed to show the moral courage of a Scottish patriot.
Sir Compton MacKenzie, *novelist, dedicating his book* Of Moral Courage *to Edinburgh character Wendy Wood*

Sean Connery is a Superscot. He is one of Scotland's finest ambassadors.
Daily Record, *1991*

Duncan just keeps hitting the net. I don't even want to discuss his value.
Glenn Hoddle, *player-manager of Swindon Town, of Duncan Shearer, 1991*

He's the best player in the world, without doubt.
Graeme Souness, *of Kenny Dalglish*

Their frugality and temperance deserves our imitation, which is indeed the foundation of that discretion we observe in them, at a time of life when our young gentlemen are half mad.
Thomas Salmon, A New Geographical & Highland Grammar, *1751*

PROMISES

We will end British Rail's monopoly.
Malcolm Rifkind, *reinforcing the Tory vow to privatise the railways, BBC Radio 4, 1992*

I thought he was a young man of promise; but it appears he was a young man of promises
A.J. Balfour, *of Winston Churchill on his entry to politics, 1899*

This morning's policy launch made it clear that we will have a Labour government this year and a Scottish Parliament next year.
Robbie Coltrane, *at a Labour Party policy launch, 1992*

Give me a girl at an impressionable age, and she is mine for life.
Muriel Spark, The Prime of Miss Jean Brodie

PROPERTY

Property has its duties as well as its rights.
Thomas Drummond (1797-1840), *engineer and statesman, 1838*

PROSPECTS

But, Sir, let me tell you, the noblest prospect which a Scotsman ever sees is the high road that leads him to England!
Dr Samuel Johnson, The Life of Samuel Johnson, *James Boswell, 1791*

PROSPERITY

Adversity is sometimes hard upon a man; but for one man who can stand prosperity there are a hundred that will stand adversity.
Thomas Carlyle

If a nation could not prosper without the enjoyment of perfect liberty and perfect justice, there is not in the world a nation which could ever have prospered.
Adam Smith, An Inquiry into the Nature and Causes of the Wealth of Nations

PROVERBS

There is a southern proverb – fine words butter no parsnips.
Sir Walter Scott, A Legend of Montrose

They talk of my drinking but never my thirst.
Scottish proverb

He that has lost a wife and sixpence, has lost sixpence.
Scottish proverb

Better eat gray bread in your youth than in your age.
Scottish proverb

Three failures and a fire make a Scotchman's fortune.
Alexander Hislop, Proverbs of Scotland, *1870*

Surfeits alay mair than swords.
Scottish proverb

All things helps (quod the Wren)
when she pished in the sea.
David Fergusson, Scottish Proverbs, *1641*

Humff hamff quod the Laird of Bamf
David Fergusson

PUBLISHING

Publishing is harder to get into than the inner rectum of the Vatican.
Gerard Kelly, *actor,* City Lights, *1991*

His worst is better than any other person's best.
William Hazlitt *(1778-1830), essayist, praising the work of Sir Walter Scott*

Now, Barabbus was a publisher.
Thomas Campbell, *attrib.*

'Tis pleasant, sure, to see one's name in print:
A book's a book, although there's nothing in't.
Lord Byron

All that mankind has done, thought, gained or been: is lying as in magic preservation in the pages of books.
Thomas Carlyle, Heroes and Hero Worship, *1840*

I have amused myself in bed writing a shocker – it has amused me to write, but whether it will amuse you to read is another matter.
John Buchan, *to his publisher, of* The Thirty-Nine Steps

If ever I'm going to write an autobiography I'll get
my ex-minder to write it, because he's got such a
good imagination.
Sheena Easton

QUALITIES

Everything has to be properly labelled – there's no
room for any cock-ups.
John Bain, manager of Scottish game firm, explaining the
quality packaging of stags' penises for export

Maybe that's why we have produced the great
drivers, from Ecurie Ecosse and the Border
Reivers, the great Jim Clark, and – maybe –
myself.
Jackie Stewart, praising the quality of roads in Scotland

A certain sense of humour at times. And also the
qualities of a Sherman tank.
Sir Norman Fowler, when asked to name the qualities
of a Tory Party chairman

QUOTATIONS

I like to have quotations ready for every occasion
– they give one's ideas so pat, and save one the
trouble of finding expression adequate to one's
feelings.
Robert Burns, 1788

RACISM

As far as I'm concerned, one of the biggest
problems facing Europe today is the rise of racism,
xenophobia and hostility towards ethnic
minorities.
George Robertson

REGRETS

Regret is a waste of time.
Lulu (singer), *admitting that she wishes she had kept
copies of her earlier songwriting work*

RELIGION

A machine for converting the heathen.
Thomas Carlyle, *of the Bible Society*

The one sad thing about football in Glasgow is the
religious bigotry between Rangers and Celtic. It's
been getting better but it's still not good.
Ally McCoist, *1993*

A man with God is always in the majority.
John Knox, *inscription on the Reformation Monument,
Geneva, Switzerland*

We need stronger bonds with our brothers and
sisters under God whose religious persuasion is not
Christian. Much has already been achieved in
Scotland.
Cardinal Winning, *Bishop of Glasgow, after his
elevation to Rome, 1994*

Damn
Aa.
Alexander Scott *(1920-89), poet and dramatist, 'Scotch
Religion Scotched'*

But all Scotchmen are not religious . . . some are
theologians.
Gerald Bendall, *writer, Mrs James's Bonnet, 1907*

All love is lost but upon God alone.
William Dunbar *(c.1460-c.1520), poet, 'The Merle and
the Nightingale,' c.1508*

The door opens . . . crash!
And in he comes. The Big Yin.
With the long dress and the casual sandals.
Billy Connolly, *an interpretation of the crucifixion,
1975*

Every man has a creed, but in his soul he knows
that the creed has another side.
John Buchan, 'A Lucid Interval', 1910

God was with me when I took the kick. It wasn't
my strength. It was *his* that helped score.
Brian Irvine, after taking the winning penalty for
Aberdeen in the Scottish Cup final shoot-out, 1990

Toleration is the cause of many evils, and renders
diseases or distempers in the State more strong and
powerful than any remedies.
Archibald, first Marquis of Argyll (1598-1661),
Scottish soldier and leading covenanter, on religious
tolerance, Maxims of State, 1661

An atheist is a man who has no invisible means of
support.
John Buchan

. . . and then there was Johan Cruyff, who at 35
has added a whole new meaning to the word Anno
Domini.
Archie MacPherson

REPUTATION

To some people, I am rude and aggressive – they
provoke about 50 per cent of it by their attitude to
me. I can't go around with a welcome mat around
my neck.
Sean Connery, Playboy, 1965

There are some dreadful creeps in the pop world,
and I don't suffer fools gladly.
Marlene Ross, defending her reputation as a tough
manager

Do you mind – there's a rock band here trying to
drink hot chocolate.
Donnie Monroe, revealing what he is tempted to say to
hotel guests who create a noise when the group are on tour

In a way, it doesn't matter if you are big in Europe or America – if you can't do it at home you've failed.
Texas, 1989

I trod the fairways to admire the steel and skill of the player they've tagged Mr Grumpy as he showed he's really Mr Gutsy.
Iain King, *sports writer, of Colin Montgomerie*, Sunday Mail, *1994*

REVENGE

I can assure you that there was no implicit sense of trying to take revenge on the English.
Alexander Bennett, *National Trust, speaking out against plans to create a dog loo at Culloden*, Scotsman, *1993*

What about *divorce* rather than a hit man or a hammer? Or is that too old fashioned these days?
Joan Burnie, *expressing concern at women's groups who advocate unorthodox methods of revenge against men*

No more tears now; I will think upon revenge.
Mary, Queen of Scots, *on hearing of the murder of her secretary, David Riccio, by her husband, Lord Darnley*

RIVALRY

The world expects us to play second fiddle but there's no way we'll sit back and accept this. We'll make 1991 difficult for Rangers and cause an upset.
Billy McNeill, *1991*

We really feel that it is in the public's interest to know that this company is not part of the bank.
TSB (Trustee Savings Bank) spokesman, expressing the bank's views on the Tommy Sampson Band, a dance band who have marketed themselves as the TSB since 1947, 1993

Ronnie O'Sullivan is his [Stephen Hendry's] ghost of Christmas future and will scare the life out of him in the years to come.
Barry Hearn, *promoter of new snooker rival Ronnie O'Sullivan*

If that raised £5,600, can you imagine what it would have fetched if it had been blue?
Andy Cameron, *comedian and Rangers fanatic, to Cardinal Winning, referring to the cardinal's red skull cap, which he donated for charity*

The narrow squeaks that Scotchmen have had in the last two or three internationals have convinced me that English football is now quite on a par with the Scots.
The Scottish Umpire, *1887*

R O M A N C E

America is the last abode of romance and other medieval phenomena.
Eric Linklater, Juan in America

Queen's Park against Forfar – you can't get more romantic than that.
Archie MacPherson

That lofty romantic mountain on which I have so often stayed in the days of my youth, indulged meditation and felt the raptures of a soul filled with ideas of the magnificence of God and his creation.
James Boswell, *of Arthur's Seat, Edinburgh*

I stuck an elastic band on her finger.
Sam Torrance, *champion golfer, admitting that he did not have an engagement ring when he proposed to his girlfriend on the spur of the moment*

He was a romantic in an age of romantics.
Ian Bell, *biographer and journalist, of Robert Louis Stevenson,* Observer, 1992

ROYALTY

The continuous brainwashing of the plebs in the schools and the churches and the press and on television and radio creates an atmosphere of adoring stupefication.
Willie Hamilton, *of the royal family*

Why should a Hun want to dismantle a Hanoverian monarchy?
Sir Nicholas Fairbairn, *in reply to a German MP who questioned the need for a monarchy in Europe, 1992*

The Queen of Scots is this day lighter of a fair son, and I am but barren stock.
Elizabeth I *(1533-1603)*

The most insensitive and brazen pay claim made in the last 200 years.
Willie Hamilton, *attacking provisions to increase the Queen's salary, 1969*

No more tears now; I will think upon revenge.
Mary, Queen of Scots, *on hearing of the murder of her secretary, David Riccio, by her husband, Lord Darnley*

A dead woman bites not.
Lord Grey *(d.1612), Scottish nobleman, advocating the execution of Mary, Queen of Scots (attrib.)*

The tourists who come to our island take in the monarchy along with feeding the pigeons in Trafalgar Square.
Willie Hamilton, My Queen and I

RUGBY

In this emotional tumult there is something of the spirit of Bannockburn.
R.H. Bruce Lockhart, *of a Scotland* v. *England rugby international at Murrayfield, 1937*

Of course, the Australian people here are overjoyed because that puts England ahead.
Bill McLaren, *during an England* v. *Australia rugby international*

At top level you always have to prove yourself.
Gavin Hastings, *Scotland internationalist*

The clubs in Scotland are being treated like wee boys and are being starved of their earning potential by the Scottish Rugby Union.
Norrie Rowan, *former Scotland internationalist,* Edinburgh Evening News

There is a danger of portraying the Springboks as Barlinnie Special at play.
Gary Armstrong, *Scotland internationalist, of adverse media coverage of the Springboks*

SCANDAL

Scandal is merely the compassionate allowance which the gay make to the humdrum.
Saki (H.H. Munro), *Reginald at the Carlton, 1904*

Sexual harassment is too often treated as a joke – but it can be a nightmare. Sexual harassment is still rife in the legal profession.
Helena Kennedy, *barrister,* Woman Magazine, *1991*

. . . Association Football is becoming notorious for scenes and disgraceful exhibitions of ruffianism . . . the rabble will soon make it impossible for law abiding citizens to attend matches.
Scottish Athletic Journal, *1887*

A country house with nice newly bought single beds, 'excellent' meals with second helpings, choice of TV, video or satellite, bowling green.
Tom Brown, *columnist, describing a Scottish open prison, 1993*

SCOTS

Scotchmen seem to think it's a credit to them to be Scotch.
W. Somerset Maugham, A Writer's Notebook, 1949

The Scotch are a nation of gentlemen.
George IV (1762-1830)

I've been described as a Scots-born American, but make no mistake, I'm a true Scot from the top of my head to the tips of my toes.
Tom Sutherland, hostage freed from Beirut

Never before have Labour fielded so many Scots in their front line. People like John Smith, Gordon Brown, Robin Cook and Donald Dewar and 14 other tartan terrors.
Record Review, March 1992

'Guid gi'e us a guid conceit o' oursel's' is the Scotsman's most earnest prayer.
James Bridie (O.H. Mavor), One Way of Living, 1939

I think it possible that all Scots are illegitimate, Scotsmen being so mean and Scotswomen so generous.
Edwin Muir (1887-1959), poet, Scottish Journey, 1935

My lady, there are few more impressive sights in the world than a Scotsman on the make.
J.M. Barrie, What Every Woman Knows, 1908

A great Scot who's banged more baddies and Betties than humanly possible.
An American magazine's description of Sean Connery's 007

As Dr Johnson never said, is there any Scotsman without charm?
J.M. Barrie

I have been trying all my life to like Scotchmen, and am obligated to desist from the experiment in despair.
Charles Lamb (1775-1834), English essayist

And now, let us consider the Scotsman. (You will note that he is a Scotsman and that he must never be referred to as Scotch. Scotch is a drink.)
Alexander King, Rich Man, Poor Man, Freud and Fruit

Scots are so used to being in a provincial backwater that we shy clear of making claims about our potential impact upon the wider human scene. But it is time to set aside this self-effacement.
Jim Sillars, Scotland – A Case for Optimism, 1985

Dr Livingstone, I presume?
Henry Stanley, on meeting David Livingstone

I am a missionary, heart and soul. God had an only Son, and he was a missionary and a physician. A poor, poor imitation I am or wish to be. In this service I hope to live, in it, I wish to die.
David Livingstone

Mr Watson, come here – I want you.
Alexander Graham Bell, the first words to travel by wire, Boston, 10 March 1876

To Alexander Graham Bell, who has taught the deaf to speak and enabled the listening to hear speech from the Atlantic to the Rockies, I dedicate this story of my life.
Helen Keller, dedication in her book, The Story of My Life

I came out strongly as a young lady, with my hair tied to my hat.
J.M. Barrie, as a child actor in a drama group

I have amused myself in bed writing a shocker – it has amused me to write, but whether it will amuse you to read is another matter.
John Buchan, to his publisher, of The Thirty-Nine Steps

KING HAGGIS the MAGNIFICENT

I gained much general knowledge, and when I went to medical school I had a great advantage over my fellow students who were straight from school and had never got away from their books into the school of life.
Sir Alexander Fleming, *who worked as a clerk before going to medical school*

I just wouldn't know what to do with that sort of money; why, I'd not be able to sleep at night.
John Logie Baird, *when offered £125,000 for his shares in his company, Baird Television*

Sour, stingy, depressing beggars who parade around in schoolgirls' skirts with nothing on underneath.
P.J. O'Rourke, 'Foreigners Around the World', National Lampoon, 1976

If you unscotch us, you will find us damned mischievous Englishmen.
Sir Walter Scott, *letter to J.W. Crocker MP, 1826*

SCOTS FAYRE

Oats, *n.s.* A grain, which in England is generally given to horses, but in Scotland supports people.
Dr Samuel Johnson, A Dictionary of the English Language, 1735

My lords and lieges, let us all to dinner, for the cockie-leekie is a cooling.
Sir Walter Scott, The Fortunes of Nigel, 1822

Meat in Scotland is frequently kept a fortnight smothered in oat meal and carefully wiped every day.
Mrs Dalgairns, Practice in Cookery, 1829

Scotland is the best place in the world to take an appetite.
H.V. Morton, In Search of Scotland, 1929

A meal in which the Scots must be confessed to
excel at.
Dr Samuel Johnson, *of the Scottish breakfast*

SCOTLAND

The beauty of Scotland is that it is big enough to
be important in the UK, small enough for everyone
to know everyone else.
George Younger, *Conservative politician, 1982*

Scotland is obviously a very popular part of
England.
Barry Fantoni

Scotland needs the Labour Party as much as Sicily
needs the Mafia.
Malcolm Rifkind, *1992*

Scotland be Englishman's bush country.
A North African chief, 'Inside Africa', 1955

None can destroy Scotland save Scotland itself . . .
My Lord, patricide is a greater crime than
parricide.
Lord Belhaven, *opposing the Union of 1707*

Over the centuries the Scots have accepted the fact
of English domination. You've only got to look at
the figures to realise Scotland is a perpetually
depressed area. Why else do the Scots have to
leave Scotland to make a good living?
Sean Connery

SCOTLAND AND
ENGLAND

The narrow squeaks that Scotchmen have had in
the last two or three internationals have convinced
me that English football is now quite on a par
with the Scots.
The Scottish Umpire, *1887*

Seeing Scotland, Madam, is only seeing a worse
England.
Dr Samuel Johnson, letter, 1778

Scotland has suffered in the past, and is suffering
now, from too much England.
A.G. Macdonnell, My Scotland, 1937

I've sometimes thought that the difference between
the Scotch and the English is that the Scotch are
hard in all other respects but soft with women,
and the English are hard with women and soft in
all other respects.
J.M. Barrie

It would make a good prison in England.
Dr Samuel Johnson, of Edinburgh Castle

SEX

Their tricks an' craft have put me daft,
They've taen me in an' a' that
But clear your decks, and here's – 'The Sex!'
Robert Burns, 'Tho' Women's Minds Like Winter
Winds', 1790

'Sex', she says, 'is a subject like any other subject.
Every bit as interesting as agriculture.'
Muriel Spark, The Hothouse by the East River, 1973

Seriously, in the age of AIDS, could there be safer
sex?
Joan Burnie, supporting the royal toe-sucking incident,
1992

Bald heads are sexy.
Richard Wilson, actor

I don't think you can take it too seriously. Oh it's
very flattering – but the Sexiest Man Alive? There
are a few dead ones.
Sean Connery, Sunday Express Magazine, 1990

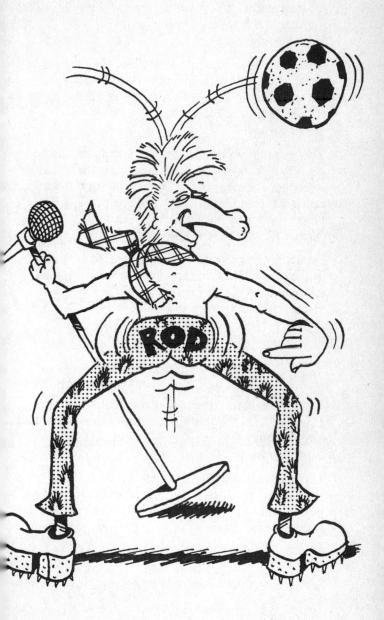

Of course a player can have sexual intercourse before a match and play a blinder. But if he did it for six months he'd be a decrepit old man. It takes the strength from the body.
Bill Shankly, 1971

What a curious, inconsistent thing is the mind of a man! In the midst of divine service I was laying plans for having women, and yet I had the most sincere feelings of religion.
James Boswell

You remember your first mountain in much the same way you remember having your first sexual experience, except that climbing doesn't make as much mess and you don't cry for a week if Ben Nevis forgets to phone the next morning.
Muriel Gray, The First Fifty, 1990

Sexual harassment is too often treated as a joke – but it can be a nightmare. Sexual harassment is still rife in the legal profession.
Helena Kennedy, Woman Magazine, 1991

SEX APPEAL

I can't speak for women, but I find Mikhail Gorbachev attractive as a man's man. It's an extraordinary combination of intelligence, baldness and serenity.
Sean Connery

Having both Wimbledon and the World Cup on at the same time is, I suppose, not unlike having a permanent skin-flick on the box. Not least when little Ms Seles comes out to play – game, set and grunt.
Joan Burnie, of Monica Seles, tennis player

It's better to be thought of as a heart-throb than as a pig.
Tom Conti

SIN

The lowest and vilest alleys of London do not present a more dreadful record of sin than does the smiling and beautiful countryside.
Sir Arthur Conan Doyle, The Adventures of Sherlock Holmes, *1891*

It does no harm to throw the occasional man overboard, but it does not do much good if you are steering full speed ahead for the rocks.
Sir Ian Gilmour, *former Cabinet minister, on being sacked by Margaret Thatcher*, Time, *1981*

A branch of the sin of drunkenness, which is the root of all sins.
James I and VI, A Counterblast to Tobacco, *1604*

SMOKING

I don't like to see a woman smoking in the streets.
Alex Smith, *manager of Aberdeen Football Club*

What are we going to do about our national disease that allows Scottish people to commit suicide and do their best at taking the rest of us with them.
Scottie McClue

It's time to say, 'stuff the smokers'. Not near me you won't. Because the little detail these pompous puffers always seem to forget is that their disgusting habit can harm others too.
Muriel Gray, *1990*

SOLITUDE

Scotland is the country above all others that I have seen, in which a man of imagination may carve out his own pleasures; there are so many *inhabited* solitudes.
Dorothy Wordsworth *(1771-1855), English writer*, Journal, *1803*

STARS

A great Scot who's banged more baddies and Betties than humanly possible.
An American magazine's description of Sean Connery's 007

Being a film star is fun. But it's not something to take all that seriously.
Emma Thompson

Charming blonde Jean Harrington plays Connie in the BBC1 series *All Creatures Great and Small*. Jean formerly played a secretary in *Crossroads* but she's recovered now, and is acting again.
Glasgow Evening Times

He's a legend.
Ian Doyle, of snooker champion Stephen Hendry, the only player to have held the World European and UK titles at the same time, 1994

She has become male Hormone Replacement Therapy and so likeable and intelligent that women can't be jealous, damn her.
Dorothy Grace Elder, television presenter and writer, of Joanna Lumley, 1995

I hope I won't always be doing it. I mean, I don't want to end up being pushed in a wheelchair singing 'Shout'.
Lulu

A man gazing at the stars is proverbially at the mercy of the puddles in the road.
Alexander Smith

As long as I am chairman, I will try to maintain the policy of signing the best available.
David Murray, defending his policy of signing high-quality football players

If he can star in front of nearly 40,000 fans at Ibrox that tells you everything about him.
Craig Brown, of Gary Smith, 1992

STYLE

Motherwell manager Tommy McLean and Hearts' Joe Jordan are still of the old tracksuits-and-trainers school.
Fiona Black, *fashion editor*, Daily Record, 1992

He wowed the Bell's Open – swathed in a Saltire jersey – as its standard-bearer. It's time he was given a break.
Sunday Mail, *of Colin Montgomerie, 1994*

The self-styled hard men like Vinny Jones don't really bother me. I've seen my fair share of dirty tricks but I can stand up for myself.
Ally McCoist

There is something about a man in a hat. I mean, where would Bogie have been without his? Just another balding bloke.
Joan Burnie, 1993

They [Scottish women] tend to be ideally suited to modelling a tattie sack with their duddies that would look more at home on nuclear warheads.
Scottie McClue, *bemoaning the fact that the average Scottish woman can't wear clothes like a supermodel*

Sir, a woman's preaching is like a dog's walking on his hinder legs. It is not done well; but you are surprised to find it done at all.
Dr Samuel Johnson, *in* Life of Johnson, *by James Boswell*

SUCCESS

To be wholly devoted to some intellectual exercise is to have succeeded in life . . .
Robert Louis Stevenson, Weir of Hermiston, *1896*

I'd like to think I've helped play a small part in their success.
Marlene Ross, *manager of Runrig*

Adversity is sometimes hard upon a man; but for one man who can stand prosperity, there are a hundred that will stand adversity.
Thomas Carlyle, Scottish author

With his clothing and his cars and his wines and his women, Bond is a kind of present-day survival kit. Men would like to imitate him – or at least, his success – and women are excited by him.
Sean Connery, Playboy, 1965

I'm just a hoary old bastard who wants to win.
Sir Ian MacGregor, Observer, 1984

Every man who is high up likes to feel he has done it all himself, and the wife smiles and lets it go at that. It's our only joke. Every woman knows that.
J.M. Barrie

It's marvellous that she stuck at it, even after getting lost.
Liz McColgan, praising the lollipop lady who came in last in the Great Scottish Run in Glasgow, 1992

The truth was that, in all those qualities which conduce to success in life, and especially in commercial life, the Scot has never been surpassed.
T.B. Macaulay, History of England

Pat and Greg Kane are at their most potent when their superb songs are stripped bare.
Billy Sloan, of Hue and Cry, 1992

What a noise. It's like being on the terraces of Tannadice.
Ricky Ross, of Deacon Blue, referring to a Belfast audience

Preparing youngsters for failure is easy; it's preparing them for success that's really difficult.
Alex Ferguson, 1991

T A L E N T

If you're anything, try to be original.
***Emma Thompson**, recalling advice given to her by her father*

I've never had that feeling of comfort with Dalglish.
***John Wile**, footballer, comparing Kenny Dalglish with other high-class opponents, 1983*

T A X E S

I have supported Scotland because I pay taxes – a full whack with none of the benefits.
Sean Connery

Lay off people who pay their poll tax.
***Malcolm Rifkind**, after discovering that the tax could increase because of non-payment by the minority, 1990*

There is no doubt that many people would like to see the Queen pay tax. Many members of the royal family are living off the taxpayers' money.
***Denis Canavan**, Labour politician*

T E C H N O L O G Y

The robot is going to lose. Not by much, but when the final score is tallied, flesh and blood is going to beat the damn monster.
Adam Smith

In the worst case, the car just becomes an unguided missile.
***David Coulthard**, Scottish driver, on Formula One technology, Scotsman, 1995*

THEATRE

Remember that the theatre of the world is wider than the realm of England.
Mary, Queen of Scots, *before her judges, 1586*

I really don't have what it takes to do Liz Taylor.
John Sessions, *of his abilities as a mimic*

Whaur's yer Wully Shakespeare noo?
Scottish theatregoer, on the first night of the Scottish play
Douglas, 1756

He is a box-office disaster, who has failed to win any awards for his production 'Honey, I Shrunk the Economy'.
John Smith, *of John Major, 1992*

He would swim through shark-infested waters to get near a microphone.
Jeremy Paxman, *television presenter and journalist, of Teddy Taylor, Conservative politician*

I think she has been lucky. Vanessa Redgrave, Maggie Smith, Judi Dench, Diana Rigg, they all have the ability to throw themselves into something completely. But Emma Thompson never loses herself.
Jack Tinker, *theatre critic, of Emma Thompson*

TIME

Those who have most to do, and are willing to work, will find the most time.
Samuel Smiles *(1812-1904), writer, Self-Help, 1859*

There's a gude time coming.
Sir Walter Scott, Rob Roy, 1817

The Berlin wall came down in a day.
Alex Salmond, *remarking on the length of time quoted by the Labour Party to set up a Scottish assembly,* Edinburgh *Evening News, 1995*

It's quite easy. She did it at four or five in the morning when she was waiting for the farming programme to come on.
Malcolm Rifkind, *to a colleague curious as to how Margaret Thatcher found time to prepare such detailed speeches, 1993*

TRAVEL

In all my travels, I never met with any one Scotsman but what was a man of sense. I believe everybody of that country that has any leaves it as fast as they can.
Dr Francis Lockler *(1667-1740), English prelate and man of letters*

To travel hopefully is a better thing than to arrive, and the true success is to labour.
Robert Louis Stevenson

On clean-shirt day he went abroad and paid visits.
James Boswell, *Scottish biographer, of Dr Johnson*

Next week we'll be looking at the Tour de France – all those bicycles roaring through the countryside.
Andy Peebles, *televison presenter*

We go where the work is. If anything, we're true Celts. The Celts have always travelled.
Jim Kerr, *admitting that he travels widely, with homes in Edinburgh, London and Dublin*

As I passed the cross, the cadies (messenger boys) and chairmen bowed and seemed to say, 'God prosper our noble Boswell.'
James Boswell, *on leaving Edinburgh for the south*

All I can add in my loneliness is, may Heaven's rich blessing come down on every one – American, English or Turk – who will help to heal this running sore of the world.
David Livingstone, *referring to Africa,* New York Herald, *1872*

I had now travelled two hundred miles in Scotland
and seen only one tree not younger than myself.
Dr Samuel Johnson, A Journey to the Western Isles of
Scotland, *1775*

We have got to start giving priority to the vehicle
carrying 87 passengers rather than the vehicle
carrying one, and three empty seats.
George Hazel, *Lothian director of highways, on
Edinburgh's transport problems, 1995*

TRUTH

Truth, like a torch, the more it's shook it shines.
Sir William Hamilton *(1788-1856), philosopher, 1852*

More people have been to the moon than have
caught HIV from a health-care professional.
Jim Johnston, *surgeon*, Scotsman, *1993*

Truth should not be spoken at all times.
Sir Walter Scott, *journal, 1827*

When you have eliminated the impossible,
whatever remains, however improbable, must be
the truth.
Sir Arthur Conan Doyle

Every man who is high up loves to feel that he has
done it all himself, and the wife smiles, and lets it
go at that. It's our only joke. Every woman knows
that.
J.M. Barrie

Poets . . . though liars by profession, always
endeavour to give an air of truth to their fictions.
David Hume, *1739*

All decent people live beyond their income
nowadays, and those who aren't respectable live
beyond other people's.
Saki (H.H. Munro), Chronicles of Clovis, *1911*

There was altogether too much candour in married life; it was an indelicate modern idea, and frequently led to upsets in a household, if not divorce.
Muriel Spark, Momento Mori, 1959

There was eternal truths, I decided, but not very many, and even these required frequent spring-cleanings.
John Buchan

Good lies need a leavening of truth to make them palatable.
William McIlvanney

VICES

Grown-ups should be allowed to go to hell with their own vices – cigarettes, cholesterol, chocolate or chips – intact.
Joan Burnie, *protesting against National No Smoking Day, 1992*

She [usually the MD's secretary] is sophisticated and unavailable until Christmas! Then sexual fireworks can explode.
Duncan McIntosh, *advising caution at the office party*

What's worn under the kilt used to be the question about Scotsmen. But now it's how can he afford to drink and smoke so much?
Iain Ferguson, *columnist, on a survey showing Scots earnings are less than a national norm,* Daily Record

We can't call ourselves a democracy as long as key national issues are decided by an unelected collection of rambling octogenarians, pensioned-off politicians and back-scratching businessmen.
Tom Brown, *of the House of Lords*

Black bottles of strong port were set down beside them on the Bench, with carafes of water, tumblers and biscuits; and this without the slightest attempt at concealment.
Lord Cockburn, *of judges on the Bench*, Memorials of His Time, *1856*

No woman should marry a teetotaller or a man who does not smoke.
Robert Louis Stevenson

We thought there was going to be a stag do, but it seems Rod prefers a hen party.
Surprised friends of Rod Stewart, on finding out that Rod was entertaining his future wife and mother-in-law before his marriage, 1993

I think the recession has a part to play in the rise in prostitution among both men and women.
Jim Murphy, *president of the National Union of Students, Scotland, 1993*

I have never considered prostitution, but at times go-go dancing can seem about as tough.
Student at Edinburgh University, 1993

Two vices especially were very prevalent, if not universal, among the upper ranks – swearing and drunkenness.
Lord Cockburn

VIRTUE

The seagreen incorruptible.
Thomas Carlyle, *of Robespierre*, History of the French Revolution

VITRIOL

Sit down, man. You're a bloody tragedy.
James Maxton *to Ramsay MacDonald, making his last speech in parliament*

More than 250 guests attended, including major friends of minor royals. Friends like Mr William Connolly, the deeply sensitive, expletive-undeleted comic.
Joan Burnie, of guests at Sting's wedding, 1992

It's a fact that women can spot a blonde hair on a man's collar across a darkened room at 2 a.m. – so why can't they see the garage doors with the headlights at full beam?
Scottie McClue

He has the precise opposite of the Midas Touch – from Black Wednesday to the pits-closure fiasco, to mysteries of whatever the government's new economic policy is, his baleful presence courts disaster.
John Smith, of John Major

A sink of atrocity, which no moral flushing seems capable of cleansing.
Lord Cockburn, of Dundee, Circuits Journeys, 1888

She is a lady short on looks, absolutely deprived of any dress sense, has a figure like a Jurassic monster, is very greedy when it comes to loot, no tact and wants to upstage everyone else. I cannot think of anybody else I would sooner not appoint to this post than the Duchess of York.
Sir Nicholas Fairbairn, *following revelations that the Foreign Office as well as Buckingham Palace were blocking moves for the Duchess to take up a high-profile appointment with the United Nations*, Evening Standard, 1993

He has sufficient conscience to bother him, but not sufficient to keep him straight.
David Lloyd-George, of Ramsay MacDonald

WAR

Defence Secretary Malcolm Rifkind is flogging off frigates in a Del Boy-style cut-price deal.
Angus Macleod, referring to the sale of warships by the Ministry of Defence, Sunday Mail, 1993

You are hereby ordered to fall upon the Rebels, the McDonalds of Glencoe, and put all to the sword under 70.
Official order for the Massacre of Glencoe, sent to Robert Campbell of Glenlyon, 1692

England should have too much artillery for the Scots.
Bill Beaumont, former England captain, before Scotland's Grand Slam victory at Murrayfield

WEALTH

No Chancellor until this one has come to the House and said that because he has money available to him the rich will get the benefits and the poor will make the sacrifices.
Gordon Brown, of Nigel Lawson's budget speech, Observer, 1988

Surplus wealth is a sacred trust which its possessor is bound to administer in his lifetime for the good of the community.
Andrew Carnegie, 'The Gospel of Wealth', North Ameican Review, 1889

The real price of every thing, what every thing really costs to the man who wants to acquire it, is the toil and trouble of acquiring it.
Adam Smith, An Inquiry in the Nature and Causes of the Wealth of Nations

Money differs from an automobile, a mistress or cancer in being equally important to those who have it and those who don't.
John Kenneth Galbraith

If a man born to a fortune cannot make himself easier and freer than those who are not, he gains nothing.
James Boswell

The increase of riches and commerce in any one nation, instead of hurting, commonly promotes the riches and commerce of all its neighbours.
David Hume

WEATHER

A Scottish mist may wet an Englishman to the skin – that is, small mischiefs in the beginning, if not seasonably prevented, may prove very dangerous.
Thomas Fuller (1608-61), *English clergyman and antiquary*, History of the Worthies of England, 1662

We surely have four seasons, sometimes in one day, in Scotland.
Jackie Stewart

The Scots are steadfast – not their clime.
Thomas Campbell (1777-1842), *poet and journalist*, The Pilgrim of Glencoe, 1842

It has been known that in the New Town of Edinburgh three or four people have been scarce able to shut the door of the house.
Edward Topham, *of the infamous Edinburgh wind*, 1774

WHISKY

I have seen a Scotchman drink three bottles of Glenlivet on a railway journey from King's Cross to Edinburgh, and when he got out at Edinburgh he strutted doucely to the refreshment bar and demanded further whisky.
T.W.H. Crosland, The Unspeakable Scot

Freedom and whisky gang the gither!
Robert Burns, 'The Author's Earnest Cry and Prayer'

The proper drinking of Scotch whisky is more than indulgence; it is a toast to civilisation, a tribute to the continuity of culture, a manifesto of man's determination to use the resources of nature to refresh mind and body and enjoy to the full the senses with which he has been endowed.
David Daiches, *critic*, Scotch Whisky, *1969*

The essential oils that wind in the glass then uncurl their long fingers in lingering benediction and the whole works of creation are made manifest. At such a moment, the basest man would bless his enemy.
Neil M. Gunn, Whisky and Scotland, *1935*

It is Sean's promotion of Japanese whisky that makes what he says so hypocritical. He has sold part of Scotland's heritage.
Willie McKelvie, *Labour politician, chairman of the All Party Scotch Whisky Group, attacking Sean Connery, 1991*

A double Scotch is about the size of a small Scotch before the war, and a single Scotch is nothing more than a dirty glass.
Lord Dundee

Whisky. For the gentlemen that like it and for the gentlemen who don't like it, whisky.
James Kennaway, *writer, 1980*

The art of making poison pleasant.
Dr Samuel Johnson, *of whisky-making*

WISDOM

A wise politician will never grudge a genuflexion or a rapture if it is expected of him by prevalent opinion.
Frederick Scott Oliver *(1864-1934), writer*

I am putting old heads on your young shoulders, and all my pupils are the crème de la crème.
Muriel Spark, The Prime of Miss Jean Brodie, *1962*

It has long been an axiom of mine that the little things are infinitely the most important.
Sir Arthur Conan Doyle

Monkeys . . . very sensibly refrain from speech, lest they should be set to earn their livings.
Kenneth Grahame

When one door opens, another smashes you in the face.
Tommy Docherty, *on his dismissal by Preston, 1981*

Some folks are wise, and some are otherwise.
Tobias Smollet

Nothing can confound a wise man more than laughter from a dunce.
Lord Byron

WIT

Crossing Piccadilly Circus
Joseph Thomson *(1858-95), explorer, in reply to J.M. Barrie, who asked what was the most hazardous part of his expedition to Africa*

WIVES

Fair, fat and forty.
Sir Walter Scott, *quoting the Prince Regent's description of a perfect wife,* St Ronan's Well

Our courtship consisted of me waiting in the lobby, then meeting him, then being taken out for a quick meal, then sitting in the committee room for a wee while. I had no illusions.
Sheila Taylor, *wife of Sir Teddy Taylor*

A seafaring man may have a sweetheart in every port; but he should steer clear of a wife as he would avoid a quicksand.
Tobias Smollett, Sir Lancellot Greaves, 1762

If the candidate has a fine woman standing by him then obviously he's going to be a dear, honest fellow. Not the kind of man who would tell lies or cheat, or have a long-running affair with a member of his staff.
Kaye Adams, *speaking out against media exposure of views of the wives of presidents, 1992*

Behind every great man is an exhausted woman.
Lady Sam Fairbairn, *wife of Sir Nicholas Fairbairn, 1994*

Do you take sugar?
Sir Ian MacGregor, *to his wife, Lady MacGregor, to whom he had been married for 45 years, but who defends such behaviour on the grounds that remembering such trivial details takes up valuable memory space, Observer, 1986*

The wife is entirely under the power and subjection of her husband.
James Balfour, *judge*, The Practiks of Sir James Balfour of Pittendreic, *1550*

WOMEN

I have always been of the opinion that none make better wives than the ladies of Scotland.
James Thomson (1700-48), *poet, letter to his sister, 1747*

I hate a woman who seems to be hermetically sealed in the lower regions.
Sydney Smith, *of an Edinburgh lady, Mrs Aprece, in* Memoir of Sydney Smith, *Lady Holland, 1855*

Women dream of falling in love with a Kwik-Fit fitter.
Tom Farmer, *founder of Kwik-Fit car repair company*, Marketing, *1989*

Women do not find it difficult nowadays to behave like men; but they often find it extremely difficult to behave like gentlemen.
Sir Compton McKenzie, On Moral Courage

I think the time has come for women – I see so
many women changing frontiers, and doing it with
good humour and with affection and with
enthusiasm, and never losing touch with their
nurturing qualities, as women who were successful
in the past often had to do. Now, it seems, one
doesn't have to abandon those things.
Helena Kennedy, *barrister and television presenter*

Women never look so well as when one comes in
wet and dirty from hunting.
Robert Louis Stevenson

All I want is Kelly.
Rod Stewart, *of his girlfriend Kelly Emberg*

Dunbar writes so scathingly of women that, when
he treats them in complimentary vein, doubts have
been cast upon his authorship.
J.W. Baxter (1465-1530), *critic, of William Dunbar*

I like a womanly woman. Nane o' your walking-
sticks for Harry Lauder!
Sir Harry Lauder, Tickling Talks

There are two things a Highlander likes naked,
and one of them is malt whisky.
Scottish proverb, The Scots Cellar

Man's the oak, woman's the ivy
J.M. Barrie, 1908

Miss Brodie was an Edinburgh spinster of the
deepest dye.
Muriel Spark, The Prime of Miss Jean Brodie, 1961

We only ask women to do two things – menstruate
and have babies – but what a fuss they make
about both.
Scottie McClue, Daily Record, 1994

If the monstrous regiment of women really is on
the march, they're going to need a good male CO.
I'm the man for the job.
Scottie McClue, 1994

WORK

Being Chancellor of the Exchequer is a humdrum activity.
Norman Lamont, Mail on Sunday, *1991*

I don't know any executive who ever thought about stress, although a lot of other people do. No one ever dies of hard work. But a lot of people die once they retire from an active job.
Sir Ian MacGregor, Daily Mail, *1980*

No, this right hand shall work it all off.
Sir Walter Scott, refusing offers of help following his bankruptcy, 1826

Women don't know what to be at next. They've tried coffee mornings and sherry parties. But what about work parties? They could tidy each other's houses so we won't find a mess behind the front door!
Scottie McClue, 1994

WORLD

You have to know a man awfully well in Canada to know his surname.
John Buchan

It is a curst, selfish, swinish country of brutes placed in the most romantic region of the world.
Lord Byron, of Switzerland

It might be called Stinkibar rather than Zanzibar.
David Livingstone, 1866

No Italian can hate the Austrians more than I do; unless it be the English, the Austrians seem to me the most obnoxious race under the sun.
Lord Byron, 1820

The simple thing is to consider the French as an erratic and brilliant people, who have all the gifts except that of running their country.
James Cameron, News Chronicle, 1954

That monstrous tuberosity of civilised life, the capital of England.
Thomas Carlyle, *of London*

I sometimes wish that I was the owner of Africa – to do at once what Wilberforce will do in time – viz. – sweep slavery from her deserts and look upon the first dance of their freedom.
Lord Byron, Detached Thoughts, *1821-2*

The world is neither Scottish, English, nor Irish, neither French, Dutch, nor Chinese, but human and each nation is only the partial development of a universal humanity.
James Grant, *on founding the National Association for the Vindication of Scottish Rights, 1852*

'World crisis' – Winston has written four volumes about himself and called it 'World Crisis'.
A.J. Balfour, *of Winston Churchill, 1899.*

X - R A T E D

Did ye hear about the Ball, my lads?
The Ball of Kirriemuir
Some came for the dancing
But they mostly cam to whore.
Sing balls to your partner,
Arse against the wall;
If you canna get fucked on a Saturday night
Ye'll never get fucked at all!
Anon., *'The Ball of Kirriemuir'*

Oh, what a peacemaker is a guid wee-willy pintle!
Robert Burns, *1788*

Women's sport, especially on TV, is really just an excuse to give some dirty old man a thrill, as they get a chance to see a flash of frilly nicks and a couple of bobbing boobs.
Joan Burnie

The Chinese are going mad for these things.
David Killoh, *manager of Scottish game firm, of stag's penises, exported to Hong Kong as an aphrodisiac, 1992*

An 'hey for houghmagandie.
Robert Burns

For the first time in my life, I would see my c**k
cut off before being unfaithful to this woman.
Rod Stewart, of his wife, Rachel Hunter, Guardian, 1992

YOUTH

I am not young enough to know everything.
J.M. Barrie

INDEX